LEGALLY
ARMED

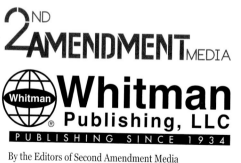

2ND
AMENDMENT MEDIA

Whitman Publishing, LLC
PUBLISHING SINCE 1934

By the Editors of Second Amendment Media

Providing Photography: Oleg Volk   Cover Image by Oleg Volk

JUL – – 2014

Correspondence concerning this book may be direct to the publisher.

Printed in the United States of America.   ISBN: 0794842070   UPC: 9780794842079

TABLE OF CONTENTS

STATES

THIS BOOK SURVEYS AND SUMMARIZES THE NATION'S GUN LAWS TO HELP KEEP YOU LEGAL.

COUNTRYMEN, FAMILY, FRIENDS AND NEIGHBORS,

Over the course of researching information for this book with my fellow editors at Second Amendment Media, I became even more aware of the vast differences in gun laws across our great, yet somewhat divided nation. It never ceases to amaze me how drastically laws differ between states and even cities within the same state. While half of our country seems bent on relaxing their states' gun laws, the other half seems just as eager to ban firearms altogether. Because of the shifting and polarizing social and political tides in our country, I've become convinced everyone who owns a gun or plans on carrying one for self-defense must have quick access to their and other states' gun laws. Simply, laws differ too drastically to go without arming yourself with knowledge, too.

Americans' varying opinions on firearm regulations reached ahead during the summer and fall of 2013, when several states passed or tried to pass a series of laws with staggeringly different agendas. On one hand, Missouri legislators passed Bill HB 436, also known as the Second Amendment Preservation Act. The bill declared residents of Missouri, among other things, would have the right to arrest federal law enforcement officers if they tried to seize an individual's firearms, regardless of make or model. The bill also obligated Missouri law enforcement officers to stop and arrest federal officers for the same reason. Thus by law, local authorities would have to intervene and confront federal agents if they tried to confiscate an individual's firearms, regardless of whether the weapon was federally prohibited. Though Governor Jay Nixon vetoed the bill before it could become law, state legislators just narrowly failed to override Nixon's veto with a two-thirds majority revote. The bill ultimately didn't pass, but the fact it almost became law is a testament to the state's extremely pro-gun disposition. Legislators in Arizona, northern parts of Colorado, Louisiana, Mississippi, North Dakota, Tennessee, Texas and Virginia have all introduced, though not necessarily passed, similar bills.

Within the same months Missouri tried to loosen its gun regulations, Maryland set into place ordinances that prohibit the future sale of certain types of semi-automatic rifles (such as AR-15s), limit guns' magazine capacities and further regulate handgun sales in the state. The laws Maryland enacted have made the state one of the most restrictive concerning carrying, owning and purchasing a weapon. Interestingly, gun sales in the state had reached an all time high in the months preceding the laws' inception and implementation. California, Colorado, Connecticut, Massachusetts, New York and New Jersey, among others, have all introduced or ratified similar bills over the last year or so.

You might find it easy ignore the vast differences between Maryland and Missouri, given their geographic distance from one another, but Vermont, one of the nation's most gun-friendly states, is a mere afternoon's drive from Maryland. Because of these states' proximity and varying stances on gun rights, every gun owner must have information on their and other states' gun laws on hand. When creating this book, we included the most essential and pertinent information for those who carry concealed weapons need to stay within the confines of the law. I ultimately hope this book provides you a piece of mind when carrying, traveling with and using your weapon in self-defense.

-The Editors of Second Amendment Media

CARRYING A FIREARM

As Americans, the freedom we have to own, use and carry firearms has remained one of our most cherished rights since our country's inception. When carefully and thoughtfully handled, firearms play an important and needed role in our country, as citizens can use them for sport, hunting and personal safety. In particular, individuals carrying a concealed weapon in public can protect themselves and others from those threatening their lives. Some skeptics believe firearms only exist to cause harm. While firearms have their dangers, those who carry concealed weapons do so to defend their own and others' right to life from those who wish to obstruct that freedom.

This book hopes to instill confidence in those who wish to go through the proper means to carry a firearm in public, and will outline how one should responsibly, safely and legally carry a weapon in each of the 50 states. The first portion of the book focuses on some of the overarching concerns and issues regarding carrying a weapon, while the latter portion details laws particular to each of the 50 states. Average citizens will often find their state's gun laws complicated and vague, but we intend to help assure and guide those who wish to provide a valuable service to their community by carrying a firearm. This book will establish some clear parameters and serve as a reference when questions arise concerning firearms carry. The book will primarily address individuals who have their carry permit and those in the process of registering for their carry permit. Additionally, we don't endorse or address unlawfully carrying a firearm and instead support individuals who carry a weapon by going through the proper legal avenues. Furthermore, one's local police department and attorney general can answer any additional questions concerning area gun laws and concealed carry regulations.

WHAT IS A CARRY PERMIT?

Typically, a concealed carry permit looks like a driver's license and doubles as a proof of identification. Once an individual obtains a carry permit, they must abide by the laws of their governing state. This book refers to those who have obtained a handgun carry permit from their state through the proper legal processes as permit holders or permit carriers. Permit holders typically have greater freedoms when handling or carrying a firearm in public than individuals who don't have their carry permit. Likewise, this book refers to those who haven't obtained a handgun carry permit as non-permit carriers, though many states still grant non-permit carriers extensive freedoms with their firearm.

Most states don't require residents to obtain a permit before purchasing a firearm, using a firearm on private lands for sporting purposes or keeping firearms in their homes. Individuals who wish to obtain a carry permit should consult their state's individual laws in the latter portion of this book or contact their local police department.

HOW TO OBTAIN A HANDGUN CARRY PERMIT

More often than not, states require training and instruction classes before awarding individuals gun carry privileges. Local outdoor agencies—such as state wildlife agencies or game and fish commissions—typically offer these classes, but local gun shops or shooting ranges may do so as well. Regardless of location, class instructors should provide citizens with an in-depth look at their state's laws and test their safety and proficiency with a firearm.

One should contact their respective state's wildlife agency, attorney general's office or local gun dealer for information regarding these permit classes. After a gun carry course awards an individual a certificate of completion, that individual may register for a gun carry permit with their state, much as one would for a driver's license or proof of identification. Additionally, most states require citizens be at least 21 years old before recieving a carry permit. Before registering for a carry permit class, one should check the age restrictions for concealed carry in their state.

CONCEALED AND UNCONCEALED FIREARMS

When considering whether one should carry a firearm, consider the difference between carrying a concealed or unconcealed (open) firearm. When brought in public, a concealed firearm should remain hidden on a person, usually by concealing the weapon under a garment or in a backpack or bag. Some states consider the indention or impression of a firearm through an article of clothing or bag as carrying an unconcealed weapon; therefore, permit carriers should ensure their firearm remains as hidden as possible when in public. A permit carrier should determine how hidden their weapon must remain to be considered fully concealed. The next chapter of this book will help determine what type of handgun new permit carriers could use as a concealed weapon.

In contrast, those carrying an unconcealed firearm wear their weapon outside their clothing, much as how law enforcement officers wear their firearms at their sides. Individuals carrying unconcealed firearms typically wear their guns on belt holsters, under the arm or on a leg holster. While some states permit carrying an unconcealed firearm, we'd generally consider doing so unwise, as the practice usually draws unwanted attention to the gun. Bystanders could even mistake a person carrying an unconcealed firearm as a member of law enforcement. Again, while laws may permit unconcealed carry, we'd encourage extreme discretion before carrying an unconcealed firearm in public.

TO SHOOT OR NOT TO SHOOT

A SITUATION: TO SHOOT OR NOT TO SHOOT

Before reading the rest of this book, consider the following scenario and try to determine the best course of action. We'll provide the answer to the scenario in chapter four, "Protecting Oneself: Discharging a Firearm in Self-Defense." Decide if a permit carrier has the right to discharge their firearm in self-defense or if doing so would be illegal. The scenario is as follows:

Your young son woke up in the middle of the night with a cold. Not having the right medicine in the house, you, trying to be a good parent, decide to drive to the neighborhood all-night pharmacy and pick up some cough syrup to help him sleep. As you drive, the streets lay empty and still, but you've brought your revolver in the front pocket of your coat for good measure, as you've recently acquired your handgun carry permit. When you get to the pharmacy, a few cars are parked in the lot, but you still get a spot close to the door. You go in, quickly find the medicine, pay and head back outside to go home. As you unlock your sedan, a stranger approaches from the far side of the vehicle, stops and says he's going to kill you. He's just across the hood of your sedan and you can't tell if he has a weapon or not. What should you do? Is your life in danger? Can you pull out your gun? Can you shoot him? These are all questions a permit holder must address in a heartbeat before they may or may not discharge their firearm in self-defense.

ARE YOU MORE JUSTIFIED TO USE YOUR WEAPON?

Now consider this, let's say the assailant says nothing and doesn't stop when he reaches your car, but rather strikes the hood of your sedan with a baseball bat. How does this change the scenario? Are you more justified to use your weapon? Again, we will work through this situation in the "Protecting Oneself" chapter of this book, but as you read, try to determine how you should properly respond.

Before delving into this book, review a few key terms to help minimize any confusion over lingo and phrases throughout this text.

- **Assailant-** An individual who wishes to do harm or misconduct to another.

- **Restricted Areas or Universally Restricted Areas-** One of the primary concerns of carrying a weapon is determining where one can carry a firearm and where they cannot. This book will mention restricted areas and universally restricted areas as locations a permit carrier cannot carry a firearm, such as a courthouse, post office, most government buildings and restaurants and bars with a posted notice. Again, laws change from state to state and one should refer to their state's entry in this book or consult their attorney general or police department to determine where they can legally carry their firearm.

- **Firearm-** A firearm is simply a gun, regardless of make, model or if it's a handgun, rifle or shotgun. For the purpose of this book, the term will typically apply to handguns, as those with their carry permit should only carry these in public.

- **Long Arms-** A long arm is a rifle or shotgun that shooters set against the shoulder when firing. At a minimum, rifles and shotguns feature barrels at least 16 and 18 inches long, respectively.

- **Handguns-** While the lengths of handguns vary,

shooters don't press these guns against the shoulder when firing. Instead, these guns require shooters to extend their arms and grip the firearm with both hands when firing. Firearms experts and historians consider semi-automatic pistols and revolvers both handguns.

- **Shall Issue-** Refers to situations in which an individual can carry a firearm in public independent of the discretion of law enforcement officers. Usually this means if an individual goes through the proper avenues of pursuing their carry permit (such as taking a carry permit class and paying the fees for a permit), the government must grant them the right to carry a firearm regardless of the opinions of law enforcement officers. In this book, the statement 'All citizens can be issued a carry permit' refers to 'shall issue' permit distribution. With that, most states also have parameters barring certain individuals from obtaining a carry permit, such as those previously convicted of a felony, those with a history of substance abuse and those involved in legal proceedings.

- **May Issue-** This term usually indicates that states retain a certain level of control and discretion regarding who they grant the right to carry a firearm in public. Thus, local sheriff offices may require those seeking a carry permit to provide just cause for why they need to carry a firearm in public. The restrictiveness of May Issue laws vary from state to state and are common in states with strict gun laws.

WHAT TO CONSIDER BEFORE CARRYING A FIREARM

When carrying a firearm, a permit carrier must consider a handful of variables, ranging from the type of firearm they should carry, where they'll carry their firearm and what restrictions they might encounter. All those interested in carrying a firearm should consider these issues and thoughtfully address each before carrying a gun in public.

WHAT KIND OF FIREARM

As mentioned, a handgun allows permit holders to discretely bring their weapon in public and easily hide it from view. When choosing what kind of firearm to bring into public, various factors and situations determine what gun would best fit an individual's specific situation. While higher caliber guns provide the firepower needed to neutralize a life-threatening situation, these guns are typically larger and harder to conceal from public view. On the other hand, smaller caliber weapons, such as a .22, might have a smaller design, but lack the firepower needed to neutralize a life-threatening situation. While any gun, regardless of caliber, would likely deter an assailant, permit holders must determine the amount of firepower needed and a firearm's ease of concealment when choosing a weapon. Before continuing, we'd like to discourage all from attempting to carry shotgun or rifle in public, as law's largely forbid it and one can't discreetly carry them on their person.

Various makes and models of handguns, regardless of caliber, have their own series of benefits and drawbacks. Firearm experts have traditionally considered revolvers, sometimes called wheel-guns for their wheel-shaped revolving cylinders, as some of the most reliable handguns available. Revolvers seldom misfire and will shoot in almost any circumstance. While reliable, revolvers offer a limited number of shots, as their cylinders only hold five or six rounds.

While some will find five or six rounds enough to neutralize a life-threatening situation, others may feel they need more shots to protect themselves. Semi-automatic pistols stand as the other type of handgun often carried by permit holders, law enforcement and military forces. Because of their higher capacity magazines, semi-auto pistols can carry more rounds, but also have more intricate designs. While still extremely reliable, some new shooters may find operating semi-autos a bit complicated and daunting. With that, permit holders should consider both revolvers and semi-autos as viable choices when choosing a handgun to carry in public.

We recommend buying a firearm from a reputable dealer, local gun shop or big box department store. An individual should consult their local attorney general's office before purchasing a firearm from a non-licensed dealer and determine the laws concerning buying and trading weapons.

WHERE YOU CAN CARRY A FIREARM

Different states allow and restrict permit holders to carry their firearms in various places. You should become familiar with these locations and determine where you plan carrying your firearm. As mentioned in the 'Helpful Terms' section of this book, most states prohibit bringing a concealed firearm to courthouses, post offices, government buildings, schools, college campuses, bars and some restaurants. Below we've listed a series of other places that may or may not welcome firearms, though laws vary from state to state.

- **National Parks-** In 2010, national parks began permitting park users to carry firearms according to each state's respective firearm carry laws. For example, if a permit holder lives in Texas, that person could carry his or her firearm into a national park in Texas because Texas allows those with firearms in their state parks. With that, an Illinois resident couldn't take their weapon into a national park because the state forbids bringing weapons into their state parks. Again, each state's laws vary and one should proceed with caution before carrying a firearm into a national park.

- **State parks-** The right to bring a firearm into state parks varies from state to state, but we'll address these laws in the latter portion of this book in each state's individual page.

- **Vehicles-** While we'll address each state's specific laws in the back of this book, most states permit any person to carry a firearm in a vehicle as long the firearm remains unloaded, locked in a case and then further locked and secured in an additional rear storage compartment, such as a trunk or a truck's tool box. Persons should also keep ammunition stored separately from their firearm while in their vehicle, though some laws remain vague concerning this issue.

- **Restaurants-** Again, many states remain vague concerning which type of restaurants permit holders can carry their firearms and in which type they cannot. The latter portion of this book will further address this issue, but permit holders should avoid bringing their weapon into establishments that primarily function as bars, such as places called "The Downtown Brewery & Bar" or "T-Bones Roadhouse & Bar." Typically laws allow concealed carry in restaurants that make the majority of their profits from food sales rather than alcohol, such as Chili's, TGI Fridays or J. Alexander's. With that, laws often ban concealed carry in any restaurant that has a 'no firearms' sign or posting. Before taking a seat at a restaurant, permit carriers may consider asking a hostess or waiter if the establishment permits concealed carry.

- **Motorhomes and RVs-** Motorhomes sometimes become issues concerning firearm carry restrictions and permissions, as they function as both vehicles and residences. Courts have upheld different stances on the matter, but permit carriers should adhere to each state's laws concerning firearms in vehicles and apply that doctrine to motorhomes and RVs.

- **Commercial Trucks-** Federal law permits truck drivers to carry firearms in a commercial truck, but they must still adhere to each state's laws concerning storing firearms in vehicles. Additionally, many trucking companies implement policies forbidding their employees to carry loaded firearms in their vehicles, though federal and state laws may consider it acceptable. Because truck drives usually remain in transit between locations, they can pass through states or cities with strict firearm laws—such as Chicago or New York City—with their gun as long as it remains locked in a case and stored away.

- **Motorcycles-** Motorcycles present an interesting set of problems when carrying a firearm. As laws typically don't address motorcycles, motorcyclists can use a back, locked compartment of a motorcycle as a substitute for a car's trunk or glove compartment. Laws usually apply to permit holders on motorcycles as they would if that person were inside a car or truck. As always, we'd suggest all those in possession of a firearm to make members of law enforcement aware of their gun during any traffic stop or similar encounter.

- **Frequency of Carrying a Firearm-** Those with their concealed carry permit should consider the importance of frequently carrying their weapon. A gun can't defend your life if it sits at home or in a car's glove box. While at times carrying a weapon may seem extreme, no one can predict when a life-threatening situation may arise. Additionally, if a permit carrier uses their firearm to defend themselves from an assailant, they could incur additional legal issues if the police or lawyers determine they only sporadically carried their firearm. These officials could assume the permit carrier premeditated the shooting and only brought the firearm in public to harm another person. Thus, we strongly urge permit carriers to regularly carry their weapon after receiving their carry permit.

WHERE YOU CAN CARRY A FIREARM

ALCOHOL

A permit carrier shouldn't consume alcohol while in possession of a firearm. If a permit carrier plans on consuming alcohol, he or she should unload their firearm, remove rounds from the magazine, separate ammunition from the gun and lock the gun and ammunition in separate locations. By separating a weapon from its ammunition, the permit carrier essentially waves their right to carry a concealed firearm and thus operates as a non-permit carrier. After the permit carrier consumes alcohol, they may still drive if their weapon and ammunition stay separated and their blood alcohol content remains below the state mandated level, such as .08 or a

ALCOHOL AND GUNS SHOULD NEVER MIX

similar figure. If law enforcement catches a permit carrier in the possession of a loaded firearm while under the influence of alcohol, the permit carrier will likely incur harsh punishments, such as losing their carry permit, significant fines, and even serve jail time. If law enforcement catches a permit carrier driving under the influence but they have dissembled or unloaded their weapon, the permit carrier will likely receive the same punishment for drinking and driving as those without a firearm. To avoid any questionable or compromising situations, we strongly recommend not consuming alcohol while in the proximity of firearms, regardless of whether a person has separated and neutralized a firearm and its ammunition.

LAW ENFORCEMENT OFFICERS, ACTIVE AND RETIRED

Federal law permits active law enforcement officers to carry a concealed firearm when traveling as long as the officer has official photo identification from their department and their department has authorized him or her to carry a firearm. Typically, law enforcement officers away from their jurisdiction must keep their firearm concealed and can't take their firearm to restricted areas, such as state buildings or courthouses. Many of the same laws apply to retired law enforcement officers, though states usually place stricter limitations on these retirees. Some of these limitations require retired police officers to have worked in their department for ten years and have been honorably discharged for said department. If planning on traveling, we'd encourage both active and retired members of law enforcement to contact the police department of where they intended to travel to ensure they don't overstep their legal boundaries.

CHAPTER 3

BEING STOPPED OR INTERACTING WITH LAW ENFORCEMENT

When dealing with law enforcement officers, permit holders can implement a handful of protocols to help a situation remain cordial and non-threatening. Law enforcement officers have stressful jobs, so following the practices listed below can prevent unwanted tension from arising when in contact with the law. These guidelines only apply to permit carriers and those legally allowed to transport a loaded firearm. Each state's page in the latter portion of this book will address whether or not individuals can transport loaded firearms in their vehicles.

• During a traffic stop or similar circumstance, a permit holder should keep their hands held firmly around the steering wheel. Before the law enforcement officer gets out of their vehicle, permit carriers should remain still and not search for their proof of insurance or registration. An officer may mistake a person moving around a vehicle as searching for a firearm. As the officer approaches, we'd encourage permit carriers to wait for the officer's instructions before reaching for paperwork or a firearm.

• Though not mandated in every state, permit carriers should let a law enforcement officer know if they have a weapon on them or in their vehicle. By doing this, the permit carrier establishes they don't intend to do harm or threaten the officer. A permit carrier should always tell an officer if they have a weapon in their glove box if that's where they've also stored their license and registration. In states that don't require persons to divulge if they their carry permit or a firearm onboard, an officer retains the right to call for backup and instruct the permit carrier, typically via megaphone, to slowly exit their vehicle and place themselves in a defusing position. In order to avoid this ordeal, those with their carry permit should

tell an officer if they have a gun in their possession and retain an open level of communication with the officer concerning the weapon. Some states require permit carriers to tell the officer if they have a weapon on them, which the back portion of this book addresses.

- After a permit carrier divulges they have a firearm onboard, an officer may—though not likely—ask for the firearm. If this occurs, the permit holder should slowly reach for the firearm and pass it to the officer with the barrel facing away from all involved, giving the officer the firearm by the grip. The officer may unload the firearm until they finish the traffic stop. We should again emphasize that permit carriers with a firearm in their possession should let an officer know exactly where they've stored their firearm in their vehicle. No one should reach for or reveal a firearm without letting an officer know beforehand.

- By following these steps, interactions with law enforcement officers should remain cordial and non-aggressive. Latter chapters of this book explain how one should address law enforcement after discharging a firearm in self-defense.

NON-PERMIT CARRIERS AND FIREARMS IN VEHICLES

In states that allow non-permit carriers to transport loaded firearms, we'd recommend anyone with a firearm in their vehicle to follow the same procedures when addressing law enforcement as previously mentioned. Laws differ, but we'd again recommend individuals without a carry permit to travel with their firearms unloaded, locked in a carry case and then further locked in the trunk or rear storage compartment. Non-permit carriers should store ammunition separately from their weapon. Also note many states don't consider glove compartments a substitute for storing a gun in a vehicle's trunk. Many of these same states don't allow non-permit holders to carry loaded firearms in their vehicles. The back half of this book includes additional information concerning non-permit holders transporting firearms.

CHAPTER 4

PROTECTING ONESELF: DISCHARGING A FIREARM IN SELF-DEFENSE

Permit carriers will face their toughest decision when deciding when they have the right and responsibility to discharge their weapon. Those with their concealed carry permit should treat this situation with the utmost respect and consideration, as a trigger pull could end a life. Permit carriers should familiarize themselves with the list that follows before carrying a weapon in public for self-defense. Again, state laws differ, but the following list should cover many of the overarching concerns of firing a weapon. These guidelines don't cover areas such as metropolitan Chicago, New York or Washington D.C., where civilians can't carry concealed firearms.

1. LIFE THREATENING

Permit carriers should only discharge a firearm when an assailant has placed someone's life in immediate danger and never for another reason, such as preventing vandalism, destruction of property or theft. Most states permit the use of deadly force until the life-threatening scenario has ceased.

Consequently, the moment a permit carrier neutralizes a threat, whether through an assailant's death or fleeing, a permit carrier no longer has the right to use their firearm against another person. A permit carrier should never chase or follow an assailant to shoot or confront them after they have fled. Additionally, laws don't consider verbal threats life-endangering and a permit carrier should only draw their weapon when an assailant jeopardizes their or another person's life.

Permit holders can use the following three qualifiers to determine if police or a jury would consider a situation life-threatening. Again, laws differ between states, but the following list should provide a solid overview of recognizing a legitimate threat.

- **Means:** Simply, does the assailant have the capability of fatally wounding or ending someone's life? Most juries would agree an assailant has the means to do harm if they have a weapon or possess more physical strength than another person.

- **Position:** While an assailant may have the means to cause harm, have they entered into a position to inflict harm on another person? For example, an assailant with a knife wouldn't have entered a position to cause harm if they remain across a large parking lot. With that, most juries would agree this same assailant would have entered into a position to cause harm if they moved within conversational distance of another person. An assailant with a firearm eschews this circumstance a bit, as guns extend the range of an assailant's position to cause harm. Often determining an assailant's position requires a fair amount of discretion and can remain somewhat vague.

- **Intent:** Does the assailant actually plan on ending a person's life or causing serious bodily harm? While a potential assailant may have entered into close proximity of a permit carrier, it doesn't necessarily mean they plan on doing harm.

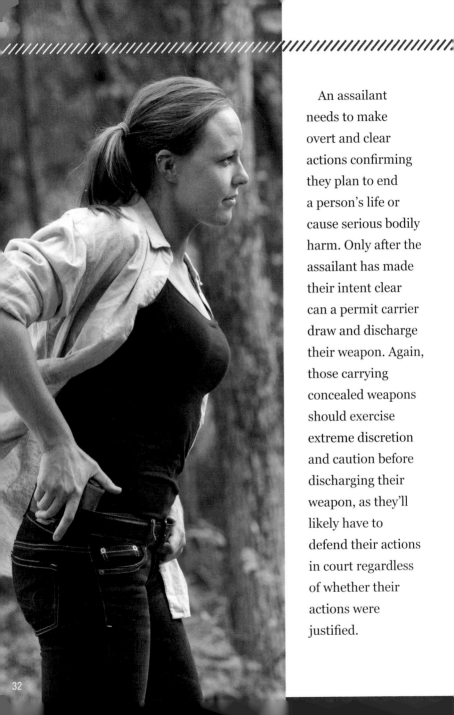

An assailant needs to make overt and clear actions confirming they plan to end a person's life or cause serious bodily harm. Only after the assailant has made their intent clear can a permit carrier draw and discharge their weapon. Again, those carrying concealed weapons should exercise extreme discretion and caution before discharging their weapon, as they'll likely have to defend their actions in court regardless of whether their actions were justified.

2. DRAWING YOUR FIREARM

A permit carrier should never draw their firearm unless prepared to fire. Thus, a permit carrier should never pull out a gun to intimidate another person or scare away a potential assailant. A permit carrier should only draw their gun the moment a threat has turned deadly and requires lethal force to neutralize. The police and a jury will not sympathize with a permit carrier who draws their firearm out of cowardice or fear of a non-existent threat.

3. ASSUMING A LAWSUIT AND RESPONSIBILITY FOR EACH BULLET

Regardless of whether their actions remain within the confines of the law, a permit carrier should assume they can and will need to defend their actions in a court of law. This means the person who discharged their weapon must establish proof they needed deadly force to defend themselves. Because of this, all permit carriers should consider the window to use their firearm in self-defense incredibly small, as a jury must support their actions. Again, permit carriers should exercise extreme discretion before using a firearm and ensure they can defend their actions under any light or angle. Along with this, the law considers permit holders, like law enforcement officers, responsible for each round fired from their gun. If a stray bullet strikes an innocent bystander, the law will likely consider the person who fired the bullet civilly responsible for any incidental injuries or death.

4. SURVEILLANCE CAMERA THEORY

Those carrying concealed weapons can use the Surveillance Camera Theory as a simple way of imagining and determining how they could defend their actions in court. When using a firearm against an assailant, a permit carrier should assume a surveillance video camera is recording their actions, as these cameras often record video and not sound. Because of this, video footage will include no verbal context of the actions occurring. Thus, if an assailant doesn't physically attack or draw a weapon against a permit holder, but the permit holder shoots the assailant, a surveillance camera will only show the shooting and not include any verbal threats made.

For example, if an assailant approached you in a parking lot and remained still and calm as they threatened your life, but you draw and fire your weapon, the cameras would only show you shooting the assailant, who would likely appear unthreatening. Most would find these actions difficult to defend in court and thus verbal threats alone can't justify using deadly force. Unfortunately, an assailant may have to draw a weapon or make a physical assault against a permit carrier before they could discharge their firearm.

5. CASTLE DOCTRINE, DUTY TO RETREAT AND STANDING YOUR GROUND

A few principles persistent across many states. Permit holders should familiarize themselves with these principles before using their firearm against another person.

- **Castle Doctrine:** A guideline set in place across a wide array of states in which individuals can use deadly force against intruders in their home. The doctrine roots itself in the thought that intruders have the means, position and likely the intent to do harm and require deadly force to neutralize. Like in defending oneself in public with deadly force, a person should assume they'll need to defend their actions in court and take responsibility for each round fired. Castle doctrine laws can differ, but remain common among gun friendly states.

- **Stand Your Ground:** More common in gun friendly states, stand your ground laws allow permit carriers to use deadly force when threatened and to not necessarily retreat or seek cover first. These laws give legal immunity to individuals who kill to protect themselves or others. Many states pair stand your ground laws with castle doctrine laws.

- **Duty to Retreat:** This standard mandates individuals should retreat from a threatening situation or conflict before using deadly force. Often this means permit holders can only use deadly force when they cannot retreat. Typically, states with stricter gun laws implement duty to retreat laws to minimize the opportunities for the use of deadly force.

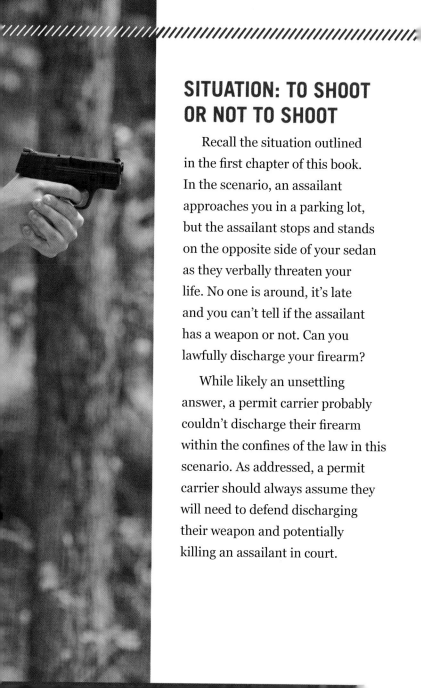

SITUATION: TO SHOOT OR NOT TO SHOOT

Recall the situation outlined in the first chapter of this book. In the scenario, an assailant approaches you in a parking lot, but the assailant stops and stands on the opposite side of your sedan as they verbally threaten your life. No one is around, it's late and you can't tell if the assailant has a weapon or not. Can you lawfully discharge your firearm?

While likely an unsettling answer, a permit carrier probably couldn't discharge their firearm within the confines of the law in this scenario. As addressed, a permit carrier should always assume they will need to defend discharging their weapon and potentially killing an assailant in court.

If you applied the Surveillance Camera Theory to this situation, you'd likely find it difficult to convince a jury an assailant placed your life in imminent danger if they didn't first draw a weapon or make an overt physical attempt against you. Before you could draw and discharge your firearm, the assailant needs to have the means, position and intent to end your or another person's life. With that, each state's laws differ as do the sympathies and alliances of the court, but even in the most gun-friendly states, most would find this a difficult case.The situation would drastically differ if the assailant drew a weapon or lunged at you with a baseball bat or similar blunt object. If this happened, most states and juries would defend discharging a weapon in self-defense.

REFLECTION

After thinking through certain concerns, a permit carrier should realize firearms provide an unparallel level of self-defense, but the scope and permissions of the law remain highly restrictive. A permit carrier should only use their firearm when an assailant has placed their or another person's life in imminent risk. Flippantly using a firearm against another or with little concern could result in murder or manslaughter charges, so we'd encourage those with their concealed carry permit to retain reverence for the law and lives of others. You should feel a healthy amount of hesitation before shooting another person in self-defense, but also recognize when such force is needed.

AFTER DISCHARGING A FIREARM

Once a permit carrier has discharged a firearm in self-defense and neutralized a threat, a new set of concerns arise that the permit carrier must address. First of all, if an assailant manages to get away after being shot or wounded, permit carriers should not chase after them and instead leave the police work to the police. If a permit carrier chases a fleeing assailant it will likely severely compromise their legal immunity regarding the shooting. After discharging a firearm and neutralizing a threat, permit carriers should implement the following steps to ensure a situation can remain as stable and controlled as possible.

1. Secure the Area- After neutralizing an assailant, whether the assailant dies or flees, the permit carrier should ensure other threats don't exist within the area.

Assailants don't always act alone when they assault or physically threaten an individual, so a permit carrier should stay alert and make sure other threats don't loom in their immediate proximity.

2. Call the Police- After or while securing and assessing the scene, call the police as soon as possible. Even if the law justifies a shooting, a permit carrier can incur heavy legal penalties if they don't immediately call the police.

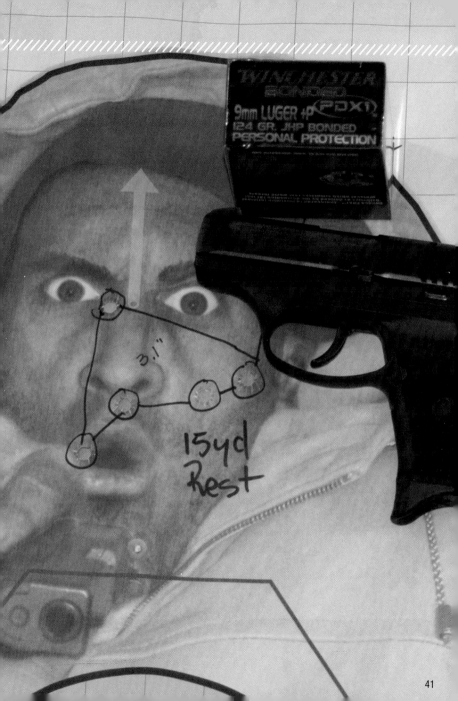

3. Set Down the Firearm-

Concurrent with calling the police, a permit carrier should set down their firearm as they wait for police to arrive. If police arrive and find a permit carrier holding a firearm, they could mistake the permit carrier for an assailant and take the appropriate action to deter the perceived threat.

Additionally, even if police can distinguish between a permit carrier and an assailant, they will treat anyone with a firearm as a threat and respond accordingly. For everyone's safety, a permit carrier should not have their firearm in hand as police arrive on the scene.

4. Watch the Firearm- After a permit holder sets their firearm on the ground, significant problems could occur if a third party takes the weapon and disappears before police arrive. As the one who's discharged a weapon, the permit carrier should guarantee their weapon doesn't vanish, as they'll likely need to use it as supportive evidence. The police, a judge or jury could wrongly assume a permit carrier hid their gun to interfere with due process or committed some wrongdoing.

5. Gather Witnesses- While waiting for the police and watching over the discharged firearm, a permit carrier should instruct others who witnessed the shooting to stay around and talk to police about what occurred. In past cases, individuals who've fired their weapon have had trouble defending their actions because of a lack of witnesses. Because of this, those who've discharged their weapon should ensure onlookers remain at the scene of the shooting. While gathering witnesses, a permit holder should also encourage these witnesses not to discuss what they've seen and instead relate all accounts directly to the police.

6. Cooperate with the Police- Once police have arrived, everyone involved should remain calm and listen to the police's instructions. Most will find shooting and potentially killing another person stressful and taxing. Because of this, the police will likely remain more collected than those involved in the shooting. If a permit holder discharges their weapon, they should only tell police pertinent information once they arrive at the scene. The permit carrier will have plenty of time to give a full account of events after the police have secured the area. We hope permit carriers use their firearm with the utmost responsibility and discretion and the police find their actions above reproach.

GUN HANDLING, PRACTICE, AND STORAGE

Before bringing a concealed firearm into public, permit carriers should familiarize themselves with how their weapon shoots, operates and requires cleaning. By becoming well versed in shooting techniques and gun maintenance, a permit carrier will find themselves better prepared if a threatening situation ever arose. This chapter will also suggest ways in which one can properly store their firearm when not carrying it in public.

HOW TO HANDLE AND SHOOT YOUR FIREARM

General Safety: When handling a firearm, a permit carrier should always treat their weapon as if it could fire at any moment. Too many people have negligently shot others after mistakenly firing their gun. Because of firearms' potential for accidental injuries, many experienced shooters treat bullets as if they were 'magic' and assume a bullet has always materialized into the chamber. This thought encourages shooters to never point a firearm at another person even if they believe they've emptied all rounds from the gun. When picking up or cleaning a firearm, one should always double and triple check the action to guarantee it remains unloaded and clear. Again, no one should ever point a firearm at an unintended target and only shoot for sport, hunting and self-defense. Additionally, no one should ever blindly shoot a target instead of carefully aiming. When a shooter walks through a field or open area with an unholstered, drawn firearm, they should also keep their firearm's barrel pointed towards the ground in case of an accidental discharge.

Trigger Finger: As shooters prepare to fire their weapon, their index finger should remain off the trigger until preparing to fire. By keeping the shooting finger off the trigger, shooters will help prevent accidental injuries and instill good habits in case they ever encountered a stressful situation. Law enforcement officers also keep their finger off the trigger until shooting, as case studies show muscles may contract unexpectedly in high intensity situations. These unanticipated muscle contractions could result in shooters pulling the trigger at the wrong time. To gauge how your motor skills could react in a high stress situation, try running wind sprints or doing pushups before firing at a target. This practice should help emphasize how easily stress can jar human reflexes and thus solidify the importance of keeping your finger off the trigger until firing.

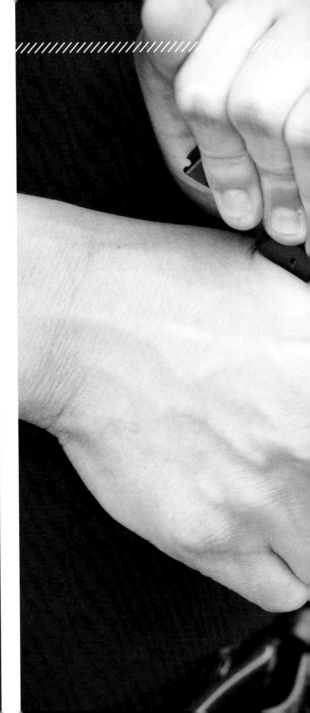

HOW TO HANDLE AND SHOOT YOUR FIREARM

CAUTION-CAPABLE OF FIRING WITH MAGAZINE REMOVED

NED5058

SMITH & WESSON
SPRINGFIELD, MA U.S.A.

49

Eyes Open: Along with keeping their finger off the trigger, law enforcement officers also leave both eyes open when aiming at a target. Case studies again show stress can cause shooters to inadvertently close both eyes while only trying to close one and aim. Closing one eye also drastically reduces peripheral vision. Law enforcement officers now train to find targets with their stronger eye, but keep both eyes open while firing. This practice will also help permit carriers prepare themselves for stressful moments.

   Grip: A firm grip also assists in careful, accurate shooting. A permit carrier or any shooter should practice drawing their weapon, firmly gripping the weapon's frame with both hands, finding their target within the sites and lowering their finger to squeeze the trigger. Practicing this routine will help shooters feel more comfortable using their weapon. Reports suggest it only takes an assailant 1.5 seconds to move 21 feet to assault a person. Because of this, permit carriers should practice quickly drawing their weapon to prevent serious injuries or even death. Again, all shooters should ensure their finger remains along the outside of their gun's frame while drawing the weapon and they only place their finger on the trigger once indentifying the target.

SHOOTING:

Below we've listed a brief checklist of shooting techniques permit carriers should master before bringing a gun in public.

- Plant both feet

- Bend the knees

- Grip the handgun in its holster

- Draw the pistol while keeping the shooting finger off the trigger

- Wrap both hands around the pistol grip with both thumbs forward along the slide

- Raise the pistol in front of the torso while facing the intended target

- Align the pistol's sights to the target

- Place the shooting finger on the trigger

- Squeeze the trigger

CLEANING AND STORAGE

Firearms, especially handguns, can misfire and malfunction when not properly cleaned. After practicing firing a weapon, any shooter should disassemble, thoroughly clean and reassemble their firearm. Most, if not all, gun shops, sporting goods stores and big box retailers carry firearm cleaning solutions or solvents. After cleaning the action and disassembling the firearm—instructions for which are included in a gun's operations manual—the person cleaning the weapon should spray cleaning solution over the gun to remove all carbon, gunpowder and skin oil residue, which could eventually cause rust. We might suggest laying a firearm on newspaper or an old towel during this process, as the residue running off the firearm can make a mess. After thoroughly spraying the gun with solvent, wipe the firearm down with a cloth or rag to remove all excess cleaning solution.

We'd suggest doing this process two or three times before putting the gun away to ensure the weapon remains as functional as possible. If using separate lubrication oil, apply the oil to all metal parts, specifically where two metal parts make contact. While cleaning a gun, approach the weapon as if it could fire at anytime and persistently check and recheck the chamber, ensuring a 'magic bullet' hasn't entered the action. Properly cleaning a firearm stands as one of the best ways a permit carrier can ensure their weapon can provide defense in a moment of conflict.

When not using or carrying a firearm, we encourage gun owners to store their weapon in a locked safe or a comparably secured location. When locked in a safe, a gun will unlikely fall into the hands of those, such as children, who may not know how to safely handle a firearm.

Gun owners should store their gun unloaded and even consider using an additional trigger lock to disable the weapon's firing mechanisms. If possible, one should store their ammunition in a separate safe or locked compartment away from their firearms. Many gun owners also have a specific firearm they keep readily accessible for home defense. While home defense is important, these guns should also stay out of reach of inexperienced shooters and children. Several manufacturers now produce small safes that open with a simple combination or fingerprint, which would make a weapon easily accessible but stored away from children.

Children are inquisitive and clever, so those with both guns and children in their homes should consider telling their children about their guns, but instruct them to never touch or look at the weapons unsupervised. Too many children have accidentally shot themselves or others after mistaking a firearm for a toy. Thus, we encourage the utmost consideration and discretion when children and firearms occupy the same home. Additionally, gun owners could also instruct all those living within proximity of their firearm—whether children or not—on how to safely and properly handle a weapon. Once a person knows how to safely handle a weapon, they become less likely to accidentally misuse it.

AVOID STORING FIREARMS IN MOIST ENVIRONMENTS, AS THIS CAN CAUSE THEM TO RUST.

TRAVELING WITH A FIREARM

Questions often arise when determining how and when a permit carrier can travel with their firearm. This section will work through some of the biggest concerns and questions and address how a permit carrier should best transport their weapon. We've included each state's particular laws on the subject, but address some overarching concerns of traveling with a firearm in this portion of the book.

Between States: By and large, neighboring states often recognize one another's handgun carry permits. Though states often recognize permits issued by one another, permit carriers must follow the laws of the state where they currently find themselves. For example, if a person with a Tennessee issued carry permit visits Arkansas, they must follow Arkansas' gun laws while in the state, not those of their native Tennessee. The same applies to individuals without their carry permit, as the laws concerning traveling with unloaded firearms also differ from state-to-state. The latter portion of this book serves as a reference for the variances in states' law so permit and non-permit carriers alike can adjust their practices accordingly. Before using the reference in the back of this book, note the term 'glove compartment' and 'vehicle storage compartment' have two distinct meanings, as 'vehicle storage compartment' indicates a compartment, such as a trunk, located outside of the passenger's riding compartment. The console between seats, a side door compartment or seat pockets also can't act as a substitute to a glove compartment; most laws don't consider these locations interchangeable in regards to storing a weapon. Additionally, 'securely encased' or 'cased' denotes those traveling with a gun must store their weapon in a commercial grade firearm case and not a handbag, backpack or duffle.

Airplanes: Concerning traveling with firearms, The Transportation Security Administration says: "Travelers may only transport UNLOADED firearms in a locked, hard-sided container in or as checked baggage. All firearms, ammunition and firearm parts, including firearm frames and receivers, are prohibited in carry-on baggage. Additionally, laws in both departing and receiving locations apply when transporting firearms on planes. Most will only find this a problem if transporting a weapon into cities that prohibit firearms, such as metropolitan Chicago or New York City. For example, New York City only allows visitors to have a locked, unloaded and cased long arm within the cities limits for 24 hours before considering them illegal. One may consult airlines and airports for further questions concerning carrying firearms to and from metropolitan cities.

Canada: To bring a handgun into Canada, a permit carrier must apply for an Authorization to Transport permit with the Canadian government. Unfortunately for Americans, Canada issues very few, if any, ATT permits to its citizens and even fewer to those from outside their country. It's unlikely worth one's time to try and obtain this type of permit. Additionally, if officials catch a person trying to unlawfully bring a handgun into the country, the government will confiscate the weapon and the culprit will likely face criminal prosecution and detainment. The same regulations apply to most military-style firearms. Though strict on handguns and assault weapons, the government will permit some foreigners to bring sporting firearms into the country after receiving a Non-Resident Firearms Declaration Form. The NRFD allows sporting rifles at least 26 inches in overall length and with barrels at least 18.5 inches in length into the country.

Those transporting sporting rifles into the country should store their guns unloaded, locked in a case, out of sight and separated from ammunition or any live rounds. Persons may only bring sporting rifles into Canada for hunting or established target shooting competitions and not for self-defense use. Gun owners should fill out the NRFD forms before trying to cross into Canada, but not sign them until reaching customs. You can obtain a NRFD form by calling 204-983-3500 or 800-731-4000. For further questions, contact the Canadian Government at www.cfc-ccaf.gc.ca/.

Mexico: Most will find bringing weapons of any sort into Mexico more difficult than bringing them into Canada, as the country forbids ownership and possession of most modern firearms and ammunition. If a gun owner does wish to bring their own firearm into the country, they should prepare to pay for an expensive Consulate Gun Permit or Military Gun Permit, along with hunting license fees. While the process remains daunting, an outfitter or hunting guide can likely help navigate the process as well as arrange for trophies to be picked up by a U.S.D.A. certified taxidermist. We recommend permit carriers or shooters rent a shotgun or rifle from a local outfitter or guide if they wish to shoot in Mexico. We don't recommend trying to bring a handgun into the country. One may further consult the Mexican Consulate at 202-736-1000 for more information.

Traveling Quick Tips:

- Attach a laminated tag with your name, address and telephone number to your gun case before checking it with luggage at the airport.

- Before flying or traveling with a gun, photograph and note the serial numbers of all your firearms in the event they get lost in transit.

- Keep guns out of sight and as discrete as possible. We wouldn't recommend leaving a firearm alone in a vehicle and would instead suggest storing them at a residence or hotel room when traveling.

- Pack guns neatly and in their most compact forms. You'll find traversing an airport or traveling in a vehicle easier if you can break down your firearm. We also suggest having the bottom of one's gun facing the hinges of their gun carry case to prevent damage to the sights if the case is dropped.

BEFORE CARRYING A FIREARM

Before reading or flipping to each state's specific entry in the back of this book, permit carriers should know this book, while accurately researched, could never include each aspect of every state's laws, given the sheer size and detail of these laws. The following pages should provide those interested in self-defense with a quick reference to some of the most basic laws they'll encounter when traveling between states. Because we hope gun carriers stay within the confines of the law, the following pages include the telephone numbers for each state's attorney general's office. If a person doesn't fully understand their rights and limitations regarding carrying, owning or buying a firearm, they can forward their questions to a state's respective attorney general. The following pages also make several assumptions, as most states have similar procedures regarding how one can obtain a concealed carry permit. We'd consider these assumptions good precautions to take if a permit carrier is unaware of their rights regarding firearms.

The assumptions include:

1.   First, to register or apply for a concealed carry permit, an individual must be at least 21 years of age or otherwise show reasonable cause to carry a firearm. Again, not all states have this law, but most states won't issue a concealed carry permit or firearm purchasing permit until an individual reaches this age.

2. For the sake of this book, we'll assume those applying for their concealed carry permit are legal residents of the state issuing the carry permit. Some states issue carry permits to individuals working in or visiting their state, but most states only issue permits to proven residents of their state. A state's attorney general can provide more information on the subject if needed. Additionally, the book mentions "all citizens" as a way of indentifying legal residents of the United States and legal residents of a respective state. No states will issue a concealed carry permit to a non-U.S. citizen.

3. Only individuals with a concealed carry or handgun permit may carry a concealed and/or unconcealed firearm. Only a few states allow individuals without a permit to carry a loaded firearm and the book notes these expectations. Usually states require a person be 21 years of age before carrying an unpermitted weapon.

4. Most states forbid firearms in: **schools, state buildings, courthouses, parades, hospitals, public sporting events, day cares, airports, banks, casinos, amusement parks, college campuses, public demonstrations, public rallies, post offices, polling places, military bases, bars and restaurants that primarily function as bars.** A permit carrier should avoid these places if unsure of local laws. It'll help you stay out of trouble! Permit carriers often struggle determining what restaurants ban firearms.

Many states allow permit carriers to dine in restaurants that earn most their money from food sales, but ban firearms from restaurants that serve alcohol or make most their profit from alcohol sales. To play it safe, a permit carrier could ask a hostess or restaurant employee if the establishment permits concealed carry or avoid the location altogether.

5. If a state doesn't recognize permits from the state that granted yours, act as if you don't have a carry permit and take the appropriate actions to operate within the confines of the law. A permit carrier shouldn't ignore a state's law because they have certain rights in other states. Thus, if you have a Tennessee issued concealed handgun permit and travel to New York City, which is a highly restrictive municipality and bans firearms, you must neutralize your firearm according to local law.

6. If a permit carrier is unsure of a state's law concerning transporting firearms, they should travel with their firearm unloaded, separated from ammunition, disassembled, locked in a commercial grade case and stored in either a trunk or out of the reach from passengers.

7. Even the strictest states (such as Illinois and Washington D.C.) allow individuals to briefly travel on the interstate through their state as long as their firearms remain secured in the manner outlined in #5. In these states, we don't recommend pulling over or spending any extended amount of time in these locations unless first contacting the state's attorney general or police department. If a permit carrier transports a weapon

forbidden in one state though another, they must ensure the firearm is legal at their destination. For example, a person may travel with a machine gun through Illinois as long as the weapon remains unloaded, disassembled, cased, locked and stored in the trunk. The person transporting the weapon may not make personal stops unrelated to travel or the law would consider the gun illegal. So, a person could stop and get gas in Illinois, but couldn't stay or even stop and visit with a family member in Chicago.

8. States often refuse individuals with felonies or certain criminal records the right to a carry a concealed weapon. These laws often apply to state's that allow the unpermitted, open carry of firearms. Individuals with felonies or pertinent criminal records should contact their lawyer or state attorney's office before applying for a concealed carry permit or carrying an unconcealed weapon in public.

9. Most states forbid firearms in restaurants and other establishments with posted signs indicating no guns.

10. When this book notes a person should keep their firearm "cased" or "locked," this means secured in a case designed to hold guns, not a gym bag, suitcase or similar storage device. Also, glove boxes and center consoles don't qualify as keeping a firearm stored in a trunk or rear compartment; states consider these legally different

We gave each state a letter and color ranking, assigning states with more relaxed laws better grades than those who impose harsher firearm restrictions. Permit holders will have greater freedoms concerning where and how they can carry their weapon in states with more favorable grades, states we consider more gun friendly.

- **A+ (Green):** These states allow permit holders maximum freedom involving how they can carry their weapon. Some of these states even allow citizens to carry an unconcealed weapon without a permit. Usually these states have stand your ground and castle doctrine laws and issue permits on a 'shall issue' basis. These states also usually recognize permits issued by other states.

- **A (Light Green):** States with A ratings still have fairly relaxed gun laws, but may further restrict where a permit carrier can have their weapon. Some of these states may also place restrictions on who they will issue permits.

- **B (Blue):** While still fairly gun friendly, these states' laws typically include specific restrictions on how one can use their weapon in self-defense. These

states may have duty to retreat laws or issue permits on a 'may issue' basis.

- **C (Yellow):** States with C grades impose fairly harsh limitations on gun ownership and carry. Usually they issue permits on a discretionary basis and don't have stand your ground or castle doctrine laws. Permit carriers should proceed with caution when traveling through these states.

- **D (Orange):** While these states may issue carry permits, they do so with extreme discretion. These states may also ban or heavily restrict the purchase and ownership of shotguns and rifles. The se states don't typically recognize carry permits issued by other states. Again, those with their carry permit or those who own a firearm of any kind should proceed with extreme caution when in these states.

- **F (Red):** These states typically don't issue or recognize any carry permits. They also usually ban firearms of any sort or place extreme restrictions on purchasing a firearm. We'd generally suggest not bringing a firearm into one of these states.

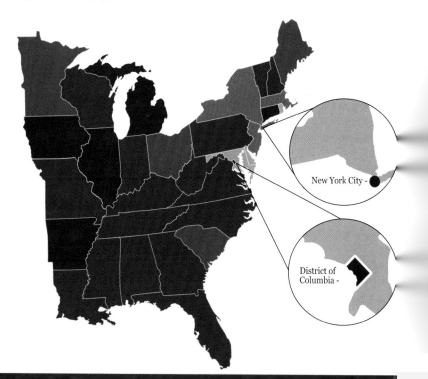

New York City -

District of Columbia -

ABAMA

Permit Carriers:

Concealed Carry: Yes, but issued by local sheriff's office for one year and might be fixed with additional restrictions

Unconcealed Carry: Yes, all citizens

Traveling with a Firearm: May transport loaded handguns and long arms

Notifying Law Enforcement of Carry Permit and Firearm: Only required if requested by an officer

Self-Defense Model: Stand your ground

Restaurants: May carry firearms in restaurants that do not have posted signs noting otherwise and as long as alcohol is not consumed.

Recognizes Carry Permits Issued by: Alaska, Arizona, Arkansas, Colorado, Florida, Georgia, Idaho, Indiana, Iowa, Kansas, Kentucky, Louisiana, Michigan, Mississippi, New Hampshire, North Carolina, North Dakota, Oklahoma, South Dakota, Tennessee, Texas, Utah, Wyoming

Law Uniformity: Local agencies cannot make additional restrictions upon state law

All Citizens and Those Without Carry Permits:

Owning a Firearm: All citizens without license or permit

Owning a Semi-Auto: All citizens without license or permit

Owning a Machine Gun: All citizens without license or permit, must abide federal law

Carrying a Loaded Firearm in Public: All citizens may carry a loaded handgun

Traveling with Firearms: Only permit carriers can transport loaded handguns. Non-permit holders must separate ammunition and store handguns cased and secured in storage compartments or trunk. All citizens may travel with long arms as long the guns remain in a gun cases or in plain view.

State Parks: Only permit carriers may carry concealed weapons

Gun Possession on College Campuses: Determined by college administration

Additional Notes and Points of Interest: Technically all citizens are allowed to carry unconcealed weapons in public without a carry permit, but this is not recommended. Only those with permits can carry concealed handguns in public. The state forbids bringing firearms to political and public demonstrations and wildlife areas.

FIREARM FRIENDLY:

Selective Excerpt From the State's Law:

Section 13A-11-59 (Locations Off Limit to Those with a Carry Permit)

Possession of firearms by individuals participating in, attending, etc., demonstrations at public places.

(a) For the purposes of this section, the following words and phrases shall have the meanings respectively ascribed to them in this subsection, except in those instances where the context clearly indicates a different meaning:

(1) DEMONSTRATION. Demonstrating, picketing, speechmaking or marching, holding of vigils and all other like forms of conduct which involve the communication or expression of views or grievances engaged in by one or more persons, the conduct of which has the effect, intent or propensity to draw a crowd or onlookers. Such term shall not include casual use of property by visitors or tourists which does not have an intent or propensity to attract a crowd or onlookers.

(2) FIREARM. Any pistol, rifle, shotgun or firearm of any kind, whether loaded or not.

(3) LAW ENFORCEMENT OFFICER. Any duly appointed and acting federal, state, county or municipal law enforcement officer, peace officer or investigating officer, or any military or militia personnel called out or directed by constituted authority to keep the law and order, and any park ranger while acting as such on the grounds of a public park and who is on regular duty and present to actively police and control the demonstration, and who is assigned this duty by his department or agency. Such term does not include a peace officer on strike or a peace officer not on duty.

Contact for Additional Information:
Attorney General of Alabama
P.O. Box 300152 • Montgomery, AL 36130
334-242-7300

Permit Carriers:

Concealed Carry: All citizens over 21 years of age, no permit required

Unconcealed Carry: All citizens over 21 years of age, no permit required

Traveling with a Firearm: All citizens over 21 years of age may transport concealed or unconcealed loaded firearms in vehicles

Notifying Law Enforcement of Carry Permit and Firearm: Immediately upon making contact with an officer

Self-Defense Model: Castle doctrine, but duty to retreat in public

Restaurants: May carry firearms in restaurants that do not have posted signs noting otherwise and as long as alcohol is not consumed.

Recognizes Carry Permits Issued by: All states

Law Uniformity: Local agencies cannot make additional restrictions upon state law

All Citizens and Those Without Carry Permits:

Owning a Firearm: All citizens without license or permit

Owning a Semi-Auto: All citizens without license or permit

Owning a Machine Gun: All citizens without license or permit, but must abide federal law

Carrying a Loaded Firearm in Public: All citizens over 21 years of age may carry a concealed handgun in public

Traveling with Firearms: All citizens over 21 years of age may transport concealed, loaded firearms in vehicles

State Parks: All non-felons

Gun Possession on College Campuses: Forbidden

Additional Notes and Points of Interest: As Alaska permits all those over 21 years of age to carry a concealed weapon in public, the only need for applying for a concealed carry permit is for those wish to travel out of state with their concealed firearm. State law also prohibits businesses from preventing employees from bringing firearms in their vehicles to work. Firearms are not permitted in bars, day cares, schools, and the homes of those who don't wish to firearms on their premise.

FIREARM FRIENDLY: A+

Selective Excerpt From the State's Law:

AS 18.65.765. Responsibilities of the permittee.

(a) The holder of a permit issued under AS 18.65.700 □ 18.65.790

(1) shall notify the department of a change in the permittee's address within 30 days;

(2) shall immediately report a lost, stolen, or illegible permit to the department;

(3) shall immediately notify the department if the holder is no longer qualified to hold a permit

under AS 18.65.705.

(4) [Repealed, Sec. 15 ch 94 SLA 2000].

(b) A person who violates this section is guilty of a violation and upon conviction may be punished by a fine of not more than $100.

Many Alaskans carry large caliber handguns, like the Magnum Research .500 JRH (shown), to defend themselves from wildlife.

Contact for Additional Information:
Alaskan State Police
5700 E. Tudor Road • Anchorage, AK 99507
907-269-0392

Permit Carriers:

Concealed Carry: All citizens shall be issued a carry permit

Unconcealed Carry: Yes, with permit

Traveling with a Firearm: All citizens with a carry permit may transport loaded handguns. Long arms should be transported unloaded.

Notifying Law Enforcement of Carry Permit and Firearm: Only required if requested by an officer

Self-Defense Model: No castle doctrine. Duty to retreat.

Restaurants: May carry firearms in restaurants that do not have posted signs noting otherwise and as long as alcohol is not consumed.

Recognizes Carry Permits Issued by: All states

Law Uniformity: Local agencies cannot make additional restrictions upon state law

All Citizens and Those Without Carry Permits:

Owning a Firearm: All citizens without license or permit

Owning a Semi-Auto: All citizens without license or permit

Owning a Machine Gun: All citizens without license or permit, must abide federal law

Carrying a Loaded Firearm in Public: Anyone at least 21 years old may carry a concealed firearm in their vehicle without a permit

Traveling with Firearms: Anyone at least 21 years old may carry a concealed firearm in their vehicle without a permit

State Parks: Only permit carriers

Gun Possession on College Campuses: Not permitted

Additional Notes and Points of Interest: While Arizona allows anyone over 21 years of age to carry a concealed weapons, individuals with carry permits are allowed greater freedoms, such as bringing their firearm into a restaurant that serves alcohol. Regardless, guns cannot be brought to schools, polling places, sports arenas, and other various public establishments.

Contact for Additional Information:
Arizona Department of Public Safety
P.O. Box 6488 • Phoenix, AZ 85005
602-256-6280

ARIZONA

Selective Excerpt From the State's Law:

13-3112. Concealed weapons; qualification; application;
permit to carry; civil penalty; report; applicability

A. The department of public safety shall issue a permit to an applicant
who meets all of the following conditions:

1. Is a resident of this state or a United States citizen.

2. Is twenty-one years of age or older.

3. Is not under indictment for and has not been convicted in any jurisdiction
of a felony unless that conviction has been expunged, set aside or vacated or
the applicant's rights have been restored and the applicant is
currently not a prohibited possessor under state or federal law.

4. Does not suffer from mental illness and has not been adjudicated mentally
incompetent or committed to a mental institution.

5. Is not unlawfully present in the United States.

6. Has ever demonstrated competence with a firearm as prescribed by
subsection N of this section and provides adequate documentation that the
person has satisfactorily completed a training program or demonstrated
competence with a firearm in any state or political subdivision in the United
States. For the purposes of this paragraph, "adequate documentation" means:

(a) A current or expired permit issued by the department of public safety
pursuant to this section.

(b) An original or copy of a certificate, card or document that shows
the applicant has ever completed any course or class prescribed by
subsection N of this section or an affidavit from the instructor, school,
club or organization that conducted or taught the course or class
attesting to the applicant's completion of the course or class.

(c) An original or a copy of a United States department of defense form 214 (DD-
214) indicating an honorable discharge or general discharge under honorable
conditions, a certificate of completion of basic training or any other document
demonstrating proof of the applicant's current or former service in the United
States armed forces as prescribed by subsection N, paragraph 5 of this section.

(d) An original or a copy of a concealed weapon, firearm or handgun permit
or a license as prescribed by subsection N, paragraph 6 of this section.

B. Notwithstanding the provisions of this section, a person with a concealed
weapons permit from another state may not carry a concealed weapon in this
state if the person is under twenty-one years of age or is under indictment for, or
has been convicted of, a felony offense in any jurisdiction, unless that conviction
is expunged, set aside or vacated or the person's rights have been restored and
the person is currently not a prohibited possessor under state or federal law.

Permit Carriers:

Concealed Carry: Yes, shall be issued to those who apply

Unconcealed Carry: Forbidden in most situations

Traveling with a Firearm: May travel with loaded handgun

Notifying Law Enforcement of Carry Permit and Firearm: Immediately upon encountering officers

Self-Defense Model: Castle doctrine, but duty to retreat in public

Restaurants: May carry firearms in restaurants that do not have posted signs noting otherwise and as long as alcohol is not consumed.

Recognizes Carry Permits Issued by: Alabama, Arizona, Arkansas, Colorado, Florida, Georgia, Idaho, Indiana, Iowa, Kentucky, Louisiana, Michigan, Mississippi, Missouri, New Hampshire, North Carolina, North Dakota, Oklahoma, South Dakota, Tennessee, Texas, Utah, and Wyoming

Law Uniformity: Local agencies cannot make additional restrictions upon state law

All Citizens and Those Without Carry Permits:

Owning a Firearm: All citizens without license or permit

Owning a Semi-Auto: All citizens without license or permit

Owning a Machine Gun: All citizens without license or permit, must abide federal law

Carrying a Loaded Firearm in Public: A firearm cannot be brought into public without a carry permit.

Traveling with Handguns: Non-permit carriers must separate ammunition and case and store handguns out of sight. Handguns cannot be stored in glove compartments.

Traveling with Long Arms: Unloaded long arms can be stored in plain view or in gun carry cases or racks.

State Parks: Permit carriers may carry concealed weapons

Gun Possession on College Campuses: Only forbidden if posted by school, but otherwise allowed by permit carriers in non-academic buildings.

Additional Notes and Points of Interest: Permits are issued to those 21 years old or over. Guns cannot be brought to college buildings, churches or places of worship, athletic stadiums and events, state buildings, and parades. A non-permit holder should never bring a firearm into public.

Contact for Additional Information:
Arkansas State Police Headquarters
1 State Police Plaza Drive • Little Rock, AR 72209
501-618-8600

FIREARM FRIENDLY: B

Selective Excerpt From the State's Law:

Section §5-73-309. License — Requirements.

The Director of the Department of Arkansas State Police shall issue a license to carry a concealed handgun if the applicant:

(1) (A) Is a resident of the state and has been a resident continuously for ninety (90) days or longer immediately preceding the filing of the application.

(B) However, subdivision (2)(A) of this section does not apply to any:

(i) Retired city, county, state, or federal law enforcement officer; or

(ii) Active duty military personnel who submit documentation of their active duty status;

(2) Does not suffer from a mental or physical infirmity that prevents the safe handling of a handgun and has not threatened or attempted suicide;

(3) (A) Has not been convicted of a felony in a court of this state, of any other state, or of the United States without having been pardoned for conviction and had firearms possession rights restored.

(B) A record of a conviction that has been sealed or expunged under Arkansas law does not render an applicant ineligible to receive a concealed handgun license if:

(i) The applicant was sentenced prior to March 13, 1995; or

(ii) The order sealing or expunging the applicant's record of conviction complies with § 16-90-605;

(4) Is not subject to any federal, state, or local law that makes it unlawful to receive, possess, or transport any firearm, and has had his or her background check successfully completed through the Department of Arkansas State Police and the Federal Bureau of Investigation's National Instant Check System;

(5) (A) Does not chronically or habitually abuse a controlled substance to the extent that his or her normal faculties are impaired.

(B) It is presumed that an applicant chronically and habitually uses a controlled substance to the extent that his or her faculties are impaired if the applicant has been:

(i) Voluntarily or involuntarily committed to a treatment facility for the abuse of a controlled substance; or

(ii) Found guilty of a crime under the provisions of the Uniform Controlled Substances Act, § 5-64-101 et seq., or a similar law of any other state or the United States relating to a controlled substance within the three year period immediately preceding the date on which the application is submitted;

(6) (A) Does not chronically or habitually use an alcoholic beverage to the extent that his or her normal faculties are impaired.

(B) It is presumed that an applicant chronically and habitually uses an alcoholic beverage to the extent that his or her normal faculties are impaired if the applicant has been:

(i) Voluntarily or involuntarily committed as an alcoholic to a treatment facility; or

(ii) Convicted of two (2) or more offenses related to the use of alcohol under a law of this state or similar law of any other state

(7) Has satisfactorily completed a training course as prescribed and approved by the director; and

(8) Signs a statement of allegiance to the United States Constitution and the Arkansas Constitution.

Permit Carriers:

Concealed Carry: Yes, but sheriffs issue with discretion

Unconcealed Carry: Forbidden in most situations and in most public areas

Traveling with a Firearm: Permit carriers can travel with a loaded handgun

Notifying Law Enforcement of Carry Permit and Firearm: Only required if requested by an officer

Self-Defense Model: No castle doctrine

Restaurants: Permit carriers can carry firearms in restaurants that do not have signs posted noting otherwise and as long as alcohol is not consumed.

Recognizes Carry Permits Issued by: None

Law Uniformity: Local agencies cannot make additional restrictions upon state law

All Citizens and Those Without Carry Permits:

Owning a Firearm: New residents must register handguns

Owning a Semi-Auto: Very restricted, assault weapon models may not be brought into the state

Owning a Machine Gun: Forbidden

Carrying a Loaded Firearm in Public: Forbidden

Traveling with Handguns: Non-permit carriers must keep unloaded handguns locked in the trunk or storage compartment, or locked in a gun case. Handguns should not be stored in a glove box or easily accessible compartment. Long arms must be unloaded but not necessarily locked in a case.

State Parks: Unlocked firearms must be cased and kept within a campsite or vehicle separated from ammunition

Gun Possession on College Campuses: Forbidden except with CA carry permit

Additional Notes and Points of Interest: The state has very strict gun laws and permit carriers should be familiarized with the law before carrying a gun in public. Unconcealed carry is almost always forbidden and permit carriers should contact the state's bureau of firearms if interested in carrying an unconcealed weapon. With a carry permit, individuals can carry a concealed handgun on their person and in their vehicle. Normal restrictions, such as bringing guns into state buildings and courthouses, also apply. For a gun to be considered 'unloaded,' live rounds must be clear of the chamber and magazine.

FIREARM FRIENDLY: D

Selective Excerpt From the State's Law:

TRAVELING WITH FIREARMS IN CALIFORNIA

HANDGUNS

California Penal Code section 25610 does not prevent a citizen of the United States over 18 years of age who is not lawfully prohibited from firearm possession, and who resides or is temporarily in California, from transporting by motor vehicle any pistol, revolver, or other firearm capable of being concealed upon the person provided the firearm is unloaded and stored in a locked container.

The term "locked container" means a secure container which is fully enclosed and locked by a padlock, key lock, combination lock, or similar locking device. This includes the trunk of a motor vehicle, but does not include the utility or glove compartment. For more information, refer to California Penal Code sections 16850.

SHOTGUNS AND RIFLES

Non-concealable firearms (rifles and shotguns) are not generally covered within the provisions of California Penal Code section 25400 and therefore are not required to be transported in a locked container. However, as with any firearm, non-concealable firearms must be unloaded while they are being transported. A rifle or shotgun that is defined as an assault weapon pursuant to Penal Code sections 30510, 30515, or 30520 must be transported in accordance with Penal Code sections 16850, 25610, and 30945, subdivision (g).

REGISTERED ASSAULT WEAPONS

California Penal Code section 30945 provides that registered assault weapons may be transported only between specified locations and must be unloaded and stored in a locked container when transported.

The term "locked container" means a secure container which is fully enclosed and locked by a padlock, key lock, combination lock, or similar locking device. This includes the trunk of a motor vehicle, but does not include the utility or glove compartment. For more information, refer to California Penal Code section 16850, 25610, and 30945, subdivision (g).

Contact for Additional Information:
California Bureau of Firearms
P.O. Box 820200 • Sacramento, CA 94203-0200
916-227-7527

CALIFORNIA

USE OF LETHAL FORCE IN SELF-DEFENSE

The question of whether use of lethal force is justified in self-defense cannot be reduced to a simple list of factors. This section is based on the instructions generally given to the jury in a criminal case where self-defense is claimed and illustrates the general rules regarding the use of lethal force in self-defense.

Permissible Use of Lethal Force in Defense of Life and Body:

The killing of one person by another may be justifiable when necessary to resist the attempt to commit a forcible and life-threatening crime, provided that a reasonable person in the same or similar situation would believe that (a) the person killed intended to commit a forcible and life-threatening crime; (b) there was imminent danger of such crime being accomplished; and (c) the person acted under the belief that such force was necessary to save himself or herself or another from death or a forcible and life-threatening crime. Murder, mayhem, rape and robbery are examples of forcible and life-threatening crimes. (Pen. Code, § 197.)

Self-Defense Against Assault:

It is lawful for a person being assaulted to defend him or herself from attack if he or she has reasonable grounds for believing, and does in fact believe, that he or she will suffer bodily injury. In doing so, he or she may use such force, up to deadly force, as a reasonable person in the same or similar circumstances would believe necessary to prevent great bodily injury or death. An assault with fists does not justify use of a deadly weapon in self-defense unless the person being assaulted believes, and a reasonable person in the same or similar circumstances would also believe, that the assault is likely to inflict great bodily injury. It is lawful for a person who has grounds for believing, and does in fact believe, that great bodily injury is about to be inflicted upon another to protect the victim from attack. In so doing, the person may use such force as reasonably necessary to prevent the injury. Deadly force is only considered reasonable to prevent great bodily injury or death.

NOTE: The use of excessive force to counter an assault may result in civil or criminal penalties.

Limitations on the Use of Force in Self-Defense:

The right of self-defense ceases when there is no further danger from an assailant. Thus, where a person attacked under circumstances initially justifying self-defense renders the attacker incapable of inflicting further injuries, the law of self-defense ceases and no further force may be used. Furthermore, a person may only use the amount of force, up to deadly force, as a reasonable person in the same or similar circumstances would believe necessary to prevent imminent injury. It is important to note the use of excessive force to counter an assault may result in civil or criminal penalties. The right of self-defense is not initially available to a person who assaults another. However, if such a person attempts to stop further combat and clearly informs the adversary of his or her desire for peace but the opponent nevertheless continues the fight, the right of self-defense returns and is the same as the right of any other person being assaulted.

Protecting One's Home:

A person may defend his or her home against anyone who attempts to enter in a violent manner intending violence to any person in the home. The amount of force that may be used in resisting such entry is limited to that which would appear necessary to a reasonable person in the same or similar circumstances to resist the violent entry. A person is not bound to retreat, even though a retreat might safely be made. Individuals may resist force with force, increasing it in proportion to the intruder's persistence and violence, if the circumstances apparent to the occupant would cause a reasonable person in the same or similar situation to fear for his or her safety. The occupant may use a firearm when resisting the intruder's attempt to commit a forcible and life-threatening crime against anyone in the home provided that a reasonable person in the same or similar situation would believe that (a) the intruder intends to commit a forcible and life-threatening crime; (b) there is imminent danger of such crime being accomplished; and (c) the occupant acts under the belief that use of a firearm is necessary to save himself or herself or another from death or great bodily injury. Murder, mayhem, rape, and robbery are examples of forcible and life-threatening crimes. Any person using force intended or likely to cause death or great bodily injury within his or her residence shall be presumed to have held a reasonable fear of imminent peril of death or great bodily injury to self, family, or a member of the household when that force is used against another person, not a member of the family or household, who unlawfully and forcibly enters or has unlawfully and forcibly entered the residence and the person using the force knew or had reason to believe that an unlawful and forcible entry had occurred. Great bodily injury means a significant or substantial physical injury. (Pen. Code, § 198.5.)

NOTE: If the presumption is rebutted by contrary evidence, the occupant may be criminally liable for an unlawful assault or homicide.

Permit Carriers:

Concealed Carry: All citizens shall be issued a carry permit

Unconcealed Carry: Unrestricted but local agencies may regulate use

Traveling with a Firearm: Loaded handguns may be transported in a vehicle for self-defense purposes. Handguns can be concealed on a person or in the glove box. Long arms should be unloaded while in transport.

Notifying Law Enforcement of Carry Permit and Firearm: Only required if requested by an officer

Self-Defense Model: Castle doctrine, but duty to retreat in public

Restaurants: May carry firearms in restaurants that do not have posted signs noting otherwise and as long as alcohol is not consumed.

Recognizes Carry Permits Issued by: Alabama, Alaska, Arizona, Arkansas, Delaware, Florida, Georgia, Idaho, Indiana, Iowa, Kansas, Kentucky, Louisiana, Michigan, Mississippi, Missouri, Montana, Nebraska, New Hampshire, New Mexico, North Carolina, North Dakota, Oklahoma, Pennsylvania, South Dakota, Tennessee, Texas, Utah, Wisconsin, Wyoming

Law Uniformity: Local agencies cannot make additional restrictions to most aspects of the state's gun law

All Citizens and Those Without Carry Permits:

Owning a Firearm: All citizens without license or permit

Owning a Semi-Auto: All citizens without license or permit

Owning a Machine Gun: All citizens without license or permit, must abide federal law

Carrying a Loaded Firearm in Public: Only when hunting

Traveling with Firearms: Loaded handguns may be transported in a vehicle for self-defense purposes. Long arms should be unloaded while in transport.

State Parks: Only permit carriers

Gun Possession on College Campuses: Only permit carriers

Additional Notes and Points of Interest: The state allows visitors to keep concealed, loaded handguns anywhere in their vehicle for self-defense purposes. This law does not apply in Denver. In Denver, only those with issued permits may carry loaded handguns in their vehicle. Local communities may ban unconcealed weapon carry. Firearms transported on a motorized snow vehicle must be stored in a case and fully unloaded when transported, including rounds from the magazine.

Contact for Additional Information:
Colorado Bureau of Investigation
690 Kipling St.- Suit 3000 • Denver, CO 80215
303-239-5850

FIREARM FRIENDLY: A+

Selected Excerpts from the State's Law:

<u>18-12-203. Criteria for obtaining a permit</u>

(1) Beginning May 17, 2003, except as otherwise provided in this section, a sheriff shall issue a permit to carry a concealed handgun to an applicant who:

(a) Is a legal resident of the state of Colorado. For purposes of this part 2, a person who is a member of the armed forces and is stationed pursuant to permanent duty station orders at a military installation in this state, and a member of the person's immediate family living in Colorado, shall be deemed to be a legal resident of the state of Colorado.

(b) Is not ineligible to possess a firearm pursuant to section 18-12-108 or federal law;

(c) Has not been convicted of perjury under section 18-8-503, in relation to information provided or deliberately omitted on a permit application submitted pursuant to this part 2;

(d) (I) Does not chronically and habitually use alcoholic beverages to the extent that the applicant's normal faculties are impaired.

(II) The prohibition specified in this paragraph (e) shall not apply to an applicant who provides an affidavit, signed by a professional counselor or addiction counselor who is licensed pursuant to article 43 of title 12, C.R.S., and specializes in alcohol addiction, stating that the applicant has been evaluated by the counselor and has been determined to be a recovering alcoholic who has refrained from using alcohol for at least three years.

(e) Is not an unlawful user of or addicted to a controlled substance as defined in section 18-18-102 (5). Whether an applicant is an unlawful user of or addicted to a controlled substance shall be determined as provided in federal law and regulations.

(f) Is not subject to:

(I) A protection order issued pursuant to section 18-1-1001 or section 19-2-707, C.R.S., that is in effect at the time the application is submitted; or

(II) A permanent protection order issued pursuant to article 14 of title 13, C.R.S.; or

(III) A temporary protection order issued pursuant to article 14 of title 13, C.R.S.

(h) Demonstrates competence with a handgun by submitting:

(I) Evidence of experience with a firearm through participation in organized shooting competitions or current military service;

(II) Evidence that, at the time the application is submitted, the applicant is a certified instructor;

(III) Proof of honorable discharge from a branch of the United States armed forces within the three years preceding submittal of the application;

(IV) Proof of honorable discharge from a branch of the United States armed forces that reflects pistol qualifications obtained within the ten years preceding submittal of the application;

(V) A training certificate from a handgun training class obtained within the ten years preceding submittal of the application. The applicant shall submit the original training certificate or a photocopy thereof that includes the original signature of the class instructor. In obtaining a training certificate from a handgun training class, the applicant shall have discretion in selecting which handgun training class to complete.

Permit Carriers:

Concealed Carry: Yes, once local permit has been granted

Unconcealed Carry: Yes, but not advised

Traveling with a Firearm: All with a carry permit may travel with a weapon

Notifying Law Enforcement of Carry Permit and Firearm: Only required if requested by officer

Self-Defense Model: No castle doctrine, duty to retreat in public

Restaurants: May carry firearms in restaurants that do not have posted signs noting otherwise and as long as alcohol is not consumed.

Recognizes Carry Permits Issued by: None except when visitors transport unloaded, locked, and secured firearms into the state.

Law Uniformity: Local communities may implement additional restrictions

All Citizens and Those Without Carry Permits:

Owning a Firearm: Need license for handgun purchase

Owning a Semi-Auto: Largely forbidden with limited importation into the state

Owning a Machine Gun: Largely forbidden with limited importation into the state

Carrying a Loaded Firearm in Public: Forbidden

Traveling with Handguns: Largely forbidden, citizens of the state must have a carry permit. Those without a permit should carry all firearms unloaded, locked in a secure case, and stored in a trunk or rear storage compartment.

State Parks: Forbidden

Gun Possession on College Campuses: Dependent on college administration

Additional Notes and Points of Interest: Connecticut has very strict gun laws and is largely against gun ownership and use. Nonresidents of the state traveling into the state for sanctioned firearm competitions and collector events should store their firearms unloaded, locked in a secured case, and kept the trunk or rear compartment of a vehicle. The permit holder should also have proof of the event on hand. Those traveling into the state without already having a carry permit should contact the state for pre-registration forms. We highly advise anyone traveling into the state with a firearm to contact the state beforehand, as their laws are convoluted and highly restrictive.

Contact for Additional Information:
Connecticut Department of Public Safety
1111 Country Club Road • Middletown, CT 06457
860-685-8190

Selected Excerpts from the State's Law:

<u>2.8-1 Self-Defense and Defense of Others -- § 53a-19 (concerning discharging a weapon).</u>
Revised to June 12, 2009 (modified May 23, 2013)

The evidence in this case raises the issue of (self-defense / the defense of others). (Self-defense / The defense of others) applies to the charge[s] of <insert applicable crimes> [and the lesser included offense[s] of <insert lesser included offenses>.]

After you have considered all of the evidence in this case, if you find that the state has proved beyond a reasonable doubt each element of a crime to which (self-defense/defense of others) applies, you must go on to consider whether or not the defendant acted in (self-defense / the defense of others). In this case you must consider this defense in connection with count[s] of the information.

A person is justified in the use of force against another person that would otherwise be illegal if (he/she) is acting in the defense of (self / others). It is a complete defense to certain crimes. When, as in this case, evidence of (self-defense / the defense of others) is introduced at trial, the state must not only prove beyond a reasonable doubt all the elements of the crime charged to obtain a conviction, but must also disprove beyond a reasonable doubt that the defendant acted in (self-defense / the defense of others). If the state fails to disprove beyond a reasonable doubt that the defendant acted in (self-defense / the defense of others), you must find the defendant not guilty despite the fact that you have found the elements of the crime proved beyond a reasonable doubt. The defendant has no burden of proof whatsoever with respect to this defense.

Deadly and non-deadly physical force1

The law distinguishes non-deadly physical force from deadly physical force. "Physical force" means actual physical force or violence or superior physical strength. The term "deadly physical force" is defined by statute as physical force which can reasonably be expected to cause death or serious physical injury. Under this definition, the physical force used by the defendant need not actually have caused a death or a serious physical injury in order to be considered deadly physical force, nor need it have been expected or intended by the defendant to result in such serious consequences. Instead, what determines whether the defendant used deadly physical force is whether the force actually used by the defendant could reasonably have been expected to cause death or serious physical injury. "Physical injury" is defined by statute as impairment of physical condition or pain, and "serious physical injury" is defined as physical injury which creates a substantial risk of death, or which causes serious disfigurement, serious impairment of health or serious loss or impairment of the function of any bodily organ.

It is up to you to determine whether the defendant used deadly physical force or non-deadly physical force against <insert name of the other person>. You are to make that determination after considering all the evidence. If the state claims that the defendant used deadly physical force, the state must prove that beyond a reasonable doubt. The first question you must resolve is whether the level of force used by the defendant rises to the level of deadly physical force, or is some lower degree of physical force.

Permit Carriers:

Concealed Carry: Forbidden, not issued

Unconcealed Carry: Forbidden, not issued

Traveling with a Firearm: Weapon must be disassembled, unloaded, locked in a case, secured in a rear compartment (not glove box), and separated from ammunition.

Notifying Law Enforcement of Carry Permit and Firearm: Permits are not issued.

Self-Defense Model: No castle doctrine

Restaurants: Forbidden

Recognizes Carry Permits Issued by: The district recognizes no carry permits

Law Uniformity: Local agencies or townships cannot make additional restrictions upon state law

All Citizens and Those Without Carry Permits:

Owning a Firearm: Restricted, firearms must be stored disassembled and registered with the district. The court recently approved handgun ownership after an extensive background check and registration process is complete. Individuals wishing to obtain a permit should contact the district.

Owning a Semi-Auto: Forbidden. Anything with a 10 round clip is illegal.

Owning a Machine Gun: Forbidden. Anything with a 10 round clip is illegal.

Carrying a Loaded Firearm in Public: Forbidden

Traveling with Handguns: Weapon must be disassembled, locked, secured in a rear compartment (not glove box), and separated from ammunition. Travelers from out of the city have certain transport rights, but those rights are waved if a person makes a stop within the city.

State Parks: Forbidden

Gun Possession on College Campuses: Forbidden

Additional Notes and Points of Interest: The district is notoriously strict regarding gun ownership and use. Though the U.S. Supreme Court has ruled the district should guarantee the rights of its citizens the right to bear arms, the city has been slow implementing this ruling and makes obtaining the right to own a handgun extremely difficult. The possession of ammunition is also illegal in the city. Individuals traveling into the district with a firearm should use extreme caution and ensure their weapon is disassembled and dysfunctional as possible. It would also be wise to consult the district before entering the city with a firearm.

FIREARM FRIENDLY: F

Selective Excerpt From the State's Law:

Firearm Registration: Complete Registration Procedures

Step 1: Complete MPD's Application for Firearms Registration Certificate (PD-219).

The form is available through DC FFLs, or through FRS. You can pick up a copy at the FRS office or contact FRS to request that a form be mailed to you. Fill out the "Purchaser/Owner's Name" of the form. If you are buying a new gun, the SELLER of the gun will complete Section A of the form. The form must be signed by both the purchaser and seller in the presence of each other.

Step 2: Bring the completed PD-219 to the FRS, along with the firearm, if appropriate.

If you already own the firearm, bring the UNLOADED gun with you. If you are purchasing a firearm, the dealer cannot release the firearm to you until you have completed this process and return with a valid registration certificate. Also bring: Proof of residency in the District of Columbia (e.g., a valid DC operator's permit, DC vehicle registration card, lease agreement for a residence in the District, the deed to your home, or other legal document showing DC residency). Proof of identity. The standards for proving this are the same as at the Department of Motor Vehicles; you must provide either ONE (1) primary source document or TWO (2) secondary source documents.

**Primary Sources: ONE (1) required and must provide original document.

-Social Security Card bearing applicant's full name, social security number, and signature.

 -Social Security Administration verification printout reflecting applicant's full name and social security number.

**Secondary Sources: TWO (2) required and must provide original document.

-Payroll statement issued within the last 12 months reflecting applicant's full name and social security number.

-Valid U.S. Military discharge papers (DD-214)

-Valid health insurance card reflecting applicant's full name and social security number.

-Valid identification card issued by government agency (excluding motor vehicle issued. driver license / identification card) reflecting applicant's full name and social security number.

-IRS W-2 (wage and tax statement) issued within the last 12 months

-Original letter or correspondence from the IRS or DC Office of Tax and Revenue issued within the last 12 months

-Government-certified copy of Federal or State
tax return filed within the last two years

Gun owners should have proof that they have met the minimum
training requirement of four hours of classroom instruction and
one hour of range instruction conducted by a state-certified or
certified military firearms instructor. An affidavit signed by the
certified firearms instructor who conducted the course providing
the name, address, and phone number of the instructor and
attesting to the successful completion of the course by the applicant
will constitute proof. Firearms instructors certified by MPD can
provide this training. A current list is available on the website or
at the FRS. Training provided by firearms instructors not on this
list will be considered on a case-by-case basis if the instruction was
provided outside of the Metropolitan Washington area. An official
license or certificate provided by a government agency for the use
of a firearm will be considered on a case-by-case basis. Examples
include, but are not limited to, a license or certificate for hunting,
armed military service, or armed service as a special police officer.

NOTE: As of July 1, 2012, residents will no longer be required to take
a training course in order to register a firearm. Instead, applicants
will be required to watch a video on firearm safe handling provided
free of charge by the District, or to substantiate that he or she has
otherwise met the minimum requirements as noted above.

Step 3: Certify, in writing, that you are not legally blind.

Step 4: Take and pass a brief multiple-choice test based on information
on DC's firearms laws and regulations provided in this guide.

To pass, you must correctly answer at least 70 percent of the
questions. The exam is designed to ensure that registrants are
familiar with basic but essential information about firearms safety
and laws. Applicants may refer to this guide while taking the test.

Step 4: Pay the appropriate fees (see chart below).

Step 5: Be fingerprinted for your background check.

FIREARM FRIENDLY:

Step 6: Once the application is approved (generally within five days), the FRS will notify you.

You can pick up your registration certificate or request that it be mailed to you. If you are registering:

A firearm that you already own, your registration process is complete.

A firearm that you have just purchased, you must bring your certificate to the dealer to retrieve the gun, and your registration process is complete.

Fees must be paid at the time of application, and can be paid only by cash or money order. Money orders should be made payable to "DC Treasurer." In addition to the fees charged by the government, there are private sector fees in this process. Anyone purchasing a firearm outside of the District will need to transfer the firearm through a Federal Firearms Licensee (FFL). At the time of the printing of this guide, the current charge is $125 per firearm. Please check with the FFL to verify current charges.

Anyone registering a first firearm before July 1, 2012, is required to take a firearms safety course (see item 2d, above). The price for the course is set by the trainer, but may cost $200 or more. Please note that as of July 1, 2012, registrants will no longer be required to take this course. Instead, applicants will be required to watch a video on firearm safe handling provided free of charge by the District.

NOTE: Pursuant to D.C. Official Code § 7-1009(1), the term "blind person" means, and the term "blind" refers to, a person who is totally blind, has impaired vision of not more than 20/200 visual acuity in the better eye and for whom vision cannot be improved to better than 20/200, or who has loss of vision due wholly or in part to impairment of field vision or to other factors which affect the usefulness of vision to a like degree.

Contact for Additional Information:
Washington Metropolitan Police Dept.
300 Indiana Av. NW -5th floor • Washington D.C. 20001
202-747-9099

Permit Carriers:

Concealed Carry: Issued on discretionary basis

Unconcealed Carry: Unrestricted unless included in area law

Traveling with a Firearm: All citizens may transport concealed or unconcealed and loaded handguns. Long arms should remain unloaded and stored in cases.

Notifying Law Enforcement of Carry Permit and Firearm: Only required if requested by an officer.

Self-Defense Model: No castle doctrine, duty to retreat in public

Restaurants: May carry firearms in restaurants that do not have posted signs noting otherwise and as long as alcohol is not consumed.

Recognizes Carry Permits Issued by: Alaska, Arizona, Arkansas, Colorado, Florida, Kentucky, Maine, Michigan, Missouri, North Carolina, North Dakota, Ohio, Oklahoma, Tennessee, Texas, Utah, West Virginia

Law Uniformity: Can vary, certain laws grandfathered in some areas

All Citizens and Those Without Carry Permits:

Owning a Firearm: All citizens without license or permit

Owning a Semi-Auto: All citizens without license or permit

Owning a Machine Gun: Forbidden

Carrying a Loaded Firearm in Public: A handgun may be carried in a holster in plain view, but this is not advisable

Traveling with Firearms: All citizens may transport loaded handguns that are kept in plain view as long as they are not stored in the glove box or on the person. Long arms should be unloaded during transport and stored in a rack or case.

State Parks: Forbidden

Gun Possession on College Campuses: Not permitted

Additional Notes and Points of Interest: Like other states in the region, the state has fairly strict gun laws and a permit carrier should practice extreme caution before bringing a firearm into the state, as carrying a concealed weapon without a permit is a felony in the state. Machine guns can only be transported through the state according to McClure-Volkmer permissions. Like Connecticut, a permit carrier should likely consult Delaware's attorney general before bringing a firearm into or through the state.

DELAWARE

Selective Excerpt From the State's Law:

§ 1441. License to carry concealed deadly weapons.

(1) The person shall make application therefore in writing and file the same with the Prothonotary of the proper county, at least 15 days before the next term of the Superior Court, clearly stating that the person is of full age and that the person is desirous of being licensed to carry a concealed deadly weapon for personal protection or protection of the person's property, or both, and also stating the person's residence and occupation. The person shall submit together with such application all information necessary to conduct a criminal history background check.

(2) At the same time the person shall file, with the Prothonotary, a certificate of five respectable citizens of the county in which the applicant resides at the time of filing the application. The certificate shall clearly state that the applicant is a person of full age, sobriety and good moral character, that the applicant bears a good reputation for peace and good order in the community in which the applicant resides, and that the carrying of a concealed deadly weapon by the applicant is necessary for the protection of the applicant or the applicant's property, or both. The certificate shall be signed with the proper signatures and in the proper handwriting of each such respectable citizen.

(3) Every such applicant shall file in the office of the Prothonotary of the proper county the application verified by oath or affirmation in writing taken before an officer authorized by the laws of this State to administer the same, and shall under such verification state that the applicant's certificate and recommendation were read to or by the signers thereof and that the signatures thereto are in the proper and genuine handwriting of each. Prior to the issuance of an initial license the person shall also file with the Prothonotary, a notarized certificate signed by an instructor or authorized representative of a sponsoring agency, school, organization or institution certifying that the applicant: (i) has completed a firearms training course which contains at least the below described minimum elements; and (ii) is sponsored by a federal, state, county or municipal law enforcement agency, a college, a nationally recognized organization that customarily offers firearms training, or a firearms training school with instructors certified by a nationally recognized organization that customarily offers firearms training.

Contact for Additional Information:
Attorney General of Delaware
820 North French Street • Wilmington, DE 19801
302-577-8400

Permit Carriers:

Concealed Carry: Yes, shall be issued to all that apply

Unconcealed Carry: Yes

Traveling with a Firearm: May transport loaded handguns and long arms

Notifying Law Enforcement of Carry Permit and Firearm: only required if requested by an officer.

Self-Defense Model: Stand your ground

Restaurants: May carry firearms in restaurants that do not have posted signs noting otherwise and as long as alcohol is not consumed.

Recognizes Carry Permits Issued by: Alabama, Alaska, Arizona, Arkansas, Colorado, Delaware, Georgia, Idaho, Indiana, Iowa, Kansas, Kentucky, Louisiana, Michigan, Mississippi, Missouri, Montana, Nebraska, New Hampshire, New Mexico, North Carolina, North Dakota, Ohio, Oklahoma, Pennsylvania, South Carolina, South Dakota, Tennessee, Texas, Utah, Virginia, Washington, West Virginia, Wyoming.

Law Uniformity: Local agencies cannot make additional restrictions upon state law

All Citizens and Those Without Carry Permits:

Owning a Firearm: All citizens without license or permit

Owning a Semi-Auto: All citizens without license or permit

Owning a Machine Gun: All citizens without license or permit, must abide federal law

Carrying a Loaded Firearm in Public: Forbidden, expect on public transportation when the gun is cased and kept off the person

Traveling with Long Arms: All citizens may carry a loaded handgun in their vehicle if the gun remains cased or holstered and off their person, so stored in a bag or backpack. This law also applies to public transportation.

State Parks: Only permit carriers

Gun Possession on College Campuses: Forbidden

Additional Notes and Points of Interest: Florida is fairly gun friendly, but a carry permit still needs to be obtained before a firearm can be brought into public. While the state allows non-permit holders to carry loaded weapons in their vehicles, it's important to ensure the firearms are properly cased and not easily accessible.

FIREARM FRIENDLY:

Selective Excerpt From the State's Law:

<u>FLORIDA CONCEALED WEAPON OR FIREARM LICENSE BASIC
ELIGIBILITY REQUIREMENTS AND DISQUALIFYING CONDITIONS.</u>

*RESIDENCY AND AGE REQUIREMENTS

-You must be at least 21 years of age unless you are a service member, as
 defined in Section 250.01, Florida Statutes, or you are a veteran of the United
 States Armed Forces who was discharged under honorable conditions.

-Unless you are serving overseas in the United States Armed Forces, you
 must CURRENTLY RESIDE in the UNITED STATES (U.S.) AND be a U.S.
 CITIZEN OR DEEMED A LAWFUL PERMANENT RESIDENT ALIEN
 by Department of Homeland Security, U.S. Citizenship and Immigration
 Service (USCIS). If you are serving overseas in the U.S. Armed Forces,
 submit a copy of your deployment documentation with your application.
 If you are not a U.S. citizen, submit documentation issued by the USCIS
 proving you are a permanent legal resident alien with proof you have
 resided in the state of residence (as shown on your application) for at
 least 90 consecutive days prior to the date the application is submitted.

 Proof of residence includes, but is not limited to:

 1. Monthly utility, telephone, power, or cable
 bills, which show your name and address.

 2. Monthly pay stubs or other documentation from your
 employer, which show your name and address.

 3. Monthly credit card statements, which show your name and address.

*YOU MUST BE ABLE TO DEMONSTRATE
 COMPETENCY WITH A FIREARM

*DISQUALIFYING CRIMES: FELONY CONVICTIONS,
 MISDEMEANOR VIOLENCE (not domestic violence), DOMESTIC
 VIOLENCE, JUVENILE OFFENSES, SUBSTANCE AND
 ALCOHOL ABUSE, MENTAL HEALTH HISTORY

Contact for Additional Information:
Florida Bureau of License Issuance
P.O. Box 6687 • Tallahassee, FL 32314-6687
850-245-5691

Permit Carriers:

Concealed Carry: Yes, shall be issued to all that apply

Unconcealed Carry: Yes

Traveling with a Firearm: May transport loaded handguns and long arms

Notifying Law Enforcement of Carry Permit and Firearm: Only required if requested by an officer.

Self-Defense Model: Castle doctrine and stand your ground

Restaurants: May carry firearms in restaurants that do not have posted signs noting otherwise and as long as alcohol is not consumed.

Recognizes Carry Permits Issued by: Alabama, Alaska, Arizona, Arkansas, Colorado, Florida, Idaho, Indiana, Iowa, Kentucky, Louisiana, Michigan, Mississippi, Missouri, Montana, New Hampshire, North Carolina, North Dakota, Oklahoma, Pennsylvania, South Dakota, Tennessee, Texas, Utah, Wisconsin, Wyoming

Law Uniformity: Local agencies cannot make additional restrictions upon state law

All Citizens and Those Without Carry Permits:

Owning a Firearm: All citizens without license or permit

Owning a Semi-Auto: All citizens without license or permit

Owning a Machine Gun: All citizens without license or permit, must abide federal law

Carrying a Loaded Firearm in Public: Individuals may carry a long arm in public as long as the weapon remains in full sight. This applies both to individuals with and without their carry permit.

Traveling with a Firearm: Loaded firearms may be stored and kept anywhere in a person's own vehicle.

State Parks: Only permit carriers

Gun Possession on College Campuses: Forbidden

Additional Notes and Points of Interest: Handguns may not be carried in churches, bars, colleges, and state buildings. As long as the hunter has the proper sporting license, hunters may carry handguns on their person without a carry permit while pursuing game. Again, all those who are not specifically prohibited from carrying a firearm may have a loaded firearm in their vehicle, residence, or business. Like most states, residents must be 21 years old or over before applying for a carry permit.

FIREARM FRIENDLY:

Selective Excerpt From the State's Law:

State laws concerning carrying a weapon (courtesy of the state's website).

What You Should Know:

While you may legally store your firearm in your home, motor vehicle or place of business without holding a license, you must apply for a license with your county probate court if you intend to carry it outside of your own property. If you carry your gun for hunting or sporting, your current hunting license permits you carry your firearm outside of your own property.

You may be guilty of a misdemeanor if you: Don't have a current firearms or hunting license when you carry a gun outside your own property. Intentionally and without legal justification point or aim a gun or pistol at another, regardless of whether the gun or pistol is loaded. Fire a gun or pistol within 50 yards of a public highway or street without legal justification for doing so. Carry a firearm into a government building, courthouse, jail or prison, state mental health facility, bar, nuclear power facility, place of worship or polling place. Discharge a firearm on private property without the approval of the property owner. Discharge a firearm while you are intoxicated. When hunting, you may be guilty of a misdemeanor if you use a weapon in a way that disregards and endangers the safety of another person. While these charges are pending, you'll forfeit your current license, and so you must then apply for a temporary hunting license.

You may be guilty of a felony if you:

Give a firearm to a minor for illegal purposes. This offense entails a fine of up to $5,000 or a three- to five-year prison sentence. Solicit or persuade a dealer to give a firearm to anyone other than the actual buyer. Deliberately alter or counterfeit a weapons carry license or carry an altered or counterfeit weapons carry license. This offense carries with it a one- to five-year prison sentence.

Contact for Additional Information:
Attorney General of Georgia
40 Capitol Square, SW • Atlanta, GA 30334
404-656-3300

Permit Carriers:

Concealed Carry: Issued with discretion

Unconcealed Carry: Forbiddens

Traveling with a Firearm: Yes, if permit is granted

Notifying Law Enforcement of Carry Permit and Firearm: Only required if requested by an officer

Self-Defense Model: No castle doctrine, duty to retreat in public

Restaurants: Permit carriers can carry firearms in restaurants that do not have posted signs noting otherwise and as long as alcohol is not consumed.

Recognizes Carry Permits Issued by: None

Law Uniformity: Local communities may implement additional restrictions

All Citizens and Those Without Carry Permits:

Owning a Firearm: Restrictive, firearms must be registered within three days of arrival or possession in the state

Owning a Semi-Auto: Restrictive, firearms must be registered within three days of arrival or possession in the state. Assault rifles are prohibited.

Owning a Machine Gun: Forbidden

Carrying a Loaded Firearm in Public: Forbidden

Traveling with Handguns: Largely forbidden. If a person has a valid reason for transporting a firearm, the weapon should be unloaded, locked in a case, and stored in a trunk or rear compartment away from ammunition. Please use extreme discretion before traveling with a firearm in the state.

State Parks: Firearms must remain locked and stored in a vehicle

Gun Possession on College Campuses: Dependent on college administration

Additional Notes and Points of Interest: Because of the state's strict laws, it's very difficult for a non-resident of the state to purchase a firearm in Hawaii. Additionally, the state issues very few carry permits and a person must be at least 21 years old before applying for one. Again, all firearms must be registered with the state within three days of obtaining them while purchasing a handgun requires approval permits. Like other restrictive states, we highly recommend individuals interested in possessing or using a firearm to consult the state before entering the state with a firearm.

HAWAII

Selective Excerpt From the State's Law:

§134-7 Ownership or possession prohibited, when; penalty.

(a) No person who is a fugitive from justice or is a person prohibited from possessing firearms or ammunition under federal law shall own, possess, or control any firearm or ammunition therefore.

(b) No person who is under indictment for, or has waived indictment for, or has been bound over to the circuit court for, or has been convicted in this State or elsewhere of having committed a felony, or any crime of violence, or an illegal sale of any drug shall own, possess, or control any firearm or ammunition therefore.

(c) No person who:

(1) Is or has been under treatment or counseling for addiction to, abuse of, or dependence upon any dangerous, harmful, or detrimental drug, intoxicating compound as defined in section 712-1240, or intoxicating liquor;

(2) Has been acquitted of a crime on the grounds of mental disease, disorder, or defect pursuant to section 704-411; or

(3) Is or has been diagnosed as having a significant behavioral, emotional, or mental disorders as defined by the most current diagnostic manual of the American Psychiatric Association or for treatment for organic brain syndromes; shall own, possess, or control any firearm or ammunition therefore, unless the person has been medically documented to be no longer adversely affected by the addiction, abuse, dependence, mental disease, disorder, or defect.

(d) No person who is less than 25 years old and has been adjudicated by the family court to have committed a felony, two or more crimes of violence, or an illegal sale of any drug shall own, possess or control any firearm or ammunition therefore.

Contact for Additional Information:
Attorney General of Hawaii
425 Queen Street • Honolulu, HI 96813
808-586-1500

(e) No minor who:

(1) Is or has been under treatment for addiction to any dangerous, harmful, or detrimental drug, intoxicating compound as defined in section 712-1240, or intoxicating liquor;

(2) Is a fugitive from justice; or

(3) Has been determined not to have been responsible for a criminal act or has been committed to any institution on account of a mental disease, disorder, or defect; shall own, possess, or control any firearm or ammunition therefore, unless the minor has been medically documented to be no longer adversely affected by the addiction, mental disease, disorder, or defect.

For the purposes of enforcing this section, and notwithstanding section 571-84 or any other law to the contrary, any agency within the State shall make its records relating to family court adjudications available to law enforcement officials.

(f) No person who has been restrained pursuant to an order of any court, including an ex parte order as provided in this subsection, from contacting, threatening, or physically abusing any person, shall possess, control, or transfer ownership of any firearm or ammunition therefore, so long as the protective order, restraining order, or any extension is in effect, unless the order, for good cause shown, specifically permits the possession of a firearm and ammunition. The restraining order or order of protection shall specifically include a statement that possession, control, or transfer of ownership of a firearm or ammunition by the person named in the order is prohibited. Such person shall relinquish possession and control of any firearm and ammunition owned by that person to the police department of the appropriate county for safekeeping for the duration of the order or extension thereof. In the case of an ex parte order, the affidavit or statement under oath that forms the basis for the order shall contain a statement of the facts that support a finding that the person to be restrained owns, intends to obtain or to transfer ownership of, or possesses a firearm, and that the firearm may be used to threaten, injure, or abuse any person. The ex parte order shall be effective upon service pursuant to section 586-6. At the time of service of a restraining order involving firearms and ammunition issued by any court, the police officer may take custody of any and all firearms and ammunition in plain sight, those discovered pursuant to a consensual search, and those firearms surrendered by the person restrained. If the person restrained is the registered owner of a firearm and knows the location of the firearm, but refuses to surrender the firearm or refuses to disclose the location of the firearm, the person restrained shall be guilty of a misdemeanor. In any case, when a police officer is unable to locate the firearms and ammunition either registered under this chapter or known to the person granted protection by the court, the police officer shall apply to the court for a search warrant pursuant to chapter 803 for the limited purpose of seizing the firearm and ammunition.

For the purposes of this subsection, good cause shall not be based solely upon the consideration that the person subject to restraint pursuant to an order of any court, including an ex parte order as provided for in this subsection, is required to possess or carry firearms or ammunition during the course of the person's employment. Good cause consideration may include but not be limited to the protection and safety of the person to whom a restraining order is granted.

(g) Any person disqualified from ownership, possession, control, or the right to transfer ownership of firearms and ammunition under this section shall surrender or dispose of all firearms and ammunition in compliance with section 134-7.3.

(h) Any person violating subsection (a) or (b) shall be guilty of a class C felony; provided that any felon violating subsection (b) shall be guilty of a class B felony. Any person violating subsection (c), (d), (e), (f), or (g) shall be guilty of a misdemeanor. [L 1988, c 275, pt of §2; am L 1990, c 191, §1; am L 1993, c 215, §1; am L 1994, c 204, §§6, 7; am L 1995, c 189, §§2, 26; am L 1998, c 133, §5; am L 1999, c 297, §1; am L 2000, c 127, §2; am L 2004, c 4, §1; am L 2006, c 27, §2]

Despite Hawaii's strict gun laws, the state has experienced an influx of 'gun tourism' from Japanese visitors. Because Japan strictly forbids firearms, many Japanese tourists take advantage of their time on the island to shoot weapons illegal in their home country.

Permit Carriers:

Concealed Carry: Yes, shall be issued to all those who apply

Unconcealed Carry: Unrestricted in most public areas

Traveling with a Firearm: Yes, unloaded or loaded handguns can be kept on a person while a vehicle is in operation. Long arms can also be transported loaded.

Notifying Law Enforcement of Carry Permit and Firearm: Only required if requested by an officer

Self-Defense Model: Castle doctrine, stand your ground

Restaurants: May carry firearms in restaurants that do not have posted signs noting otherwise and as long as alcohol is not consumed.

Recognizes Carry Permits Issued by: All states

Law Uniformity: Local agencies cannot make additional restrictions upon state law

All Citizens and Those Without Carry Permits:

Owning a Firearm: All citizens without license or permit

Owning a Semi-Auto: All citizens without license or permit

Owning a Machine Gun: All citizens without license or permit, must abide federal law

Carrying a Loaded Firearm in Public: Handguns in plain view may be carried on a person as long as the gun is in no way concealed. Outside of any incorporated township, handguns can be carried concealed as long as the carrier does not transport the concealed weapon in a vehicle or on a state highway.

Traveling with a Firearm: Loaded handguns may be carried in plain view so long as they remain easily viewable apart from the person, as on the dashboard, passenger seat or floorboard. Loaded long arms may also be transported in plain view. All unloaded guns can also be legally transported.

State Parks: Only permit carriers

Gun Possession on College Campuses: Determined by college administration

Additional Notes and Points of Interest: Idaho is a very gun friendly state and will even grant carry permits to non-residents. One is unlikely to experience any hassle when transporting firearms through the state as long as non-permit carriers keep loaded handguns secured and in plain view a part from their person.

Contact for Additional Information:
Attorney General of Idaho
P.O. Box 83720 • Boise, ID 83720
208-334-2400

FIREARM FRIENDLY: A+

Selective Excerpt From the State's Law:

CHAPTER 33

FIREARMS, EXPLOSIVES AND OTHER DEADLY WEAPONS 18-3302. ISSUANCE OF LICENSES TO CARRY CONCEALED WEAPONS.

(1) The sheriff of a county, on behalf of the state of Idaho, shall, within ninety (90) days after the filing of an application by any person who is not disqualified from possessing or receiving a firearm under state or federal law, issue a license to the person to carry a weapon concealed on his person within this state. For licenses issued before July 1, 2006, a license shall be valid for four (4) years from the date of issue. For licenses issued on or after July 1, 2006, a license shall be valid for five (5) years from the date of issue. The citizen's constitutional right to bear arms shall not be denied to him, unless one (1) of the following applies. He:

(a) Is ineligible to own, possess or receive a firearm under the provisions of state or federal law;

(b) Is formally charged with a crime punishable by imprisonment for a term exceeding one (1) year;

(c) Has been adjudicated guilty in any court of a crime punishable by imprisonment for a term exceeding one (1) year;

(d) Is an unlawful user of, or addicted to, marijuana or any depressant, stimulant or narcotic drug, or any other controlled substance as defined in 21 U.S.C. 802;

(e) Is currently suffering or has been adjudicated as follows, based on substantial evidence:

(i) Lacking mental capacity as defined in section 18-210, Idaho Code;

(ii) Mentally ill as defined in section 66-317, Idaho Code;

(iii) Gravely disabled as defined in section 66-317, Idaho Code; or

(iv) An incapacitated person as defined in section 15-5-101(a), Idaho Code.

(f) Is or has been discharged from the armed forces under dishonorable conditions;

(g) Is or has been adjudicated guilty of or received a withheld judgment or suspended sentence for one (1) or more crimes of violence constituting a misdemeanor, unless three (3) years have elapsed since disposition or pardon has occurred prior to the date on which the application is submitted;

(h) Has had entry of a withheld judgment for a criminal offense which would disqualify him from obtaining a concealed weapon license;

(i) Is an alien illegally in the United States;

(j) Is a person who having been a citizen of the United States has renounced his or her citizenship;

(k) Is subject to a protection order issued under chapter 63, title 39, Idaho Code, that restrains the person from harassing, stalking or threatening an intimate partner of the person or child of the intimate partner or person, or engaging in other conduct that would place an intimate partner in reasonable fear of bodily injury to the partner or child.

Permit Carriers:

Concealed Carry: The state began issuing carry permits in 2013

Unconcealed Carry: N/A

Traveling with a Firearm: Residents without a FOID card should travel with their firearms unloaded, disassembled, locked in a case, and stored in a trunk or rear compartment or a vehicles.

Notifying Law Enforcement of Carry Permit and Firearm: Only required if requested by an officer

Self-Defense Model: No castle doctrine, duty to retreat in public

Restaurants: Forbidden unless given specific permission by the state

Recognizes Carry Permits Issued by: No states

Law Uniformity: Local communities may implement additional restrictions

All Citizens and Those Without Carry Permits:

Owning a Firearm: Heavily restricted, citizens need FOID card to purchase any firearm

Owning a Semi-Auto: Heavily restricted, citizens need FOID card to purchase any firearm

Owning a Machine Gun: Forbidden

Carrying a Loaded Firearm in Public: Forbidden

Traveling with a Firearm: All firearms should be transported unloaded, disassembled as much as possible, or stored in a trunk or rear compartment of a vehicle. Guns are permitted at sanctioned gun ranges, gun shops, or for hunting purposes if a hunting license is also purchased.

State Parks: Forbidden

Gun Possession on College Campuses: Dependent on college administration

Additional Notes and Points of Interest: Illinois has very strict gun laws and is largely against gun ownership and use. Non-residents traveling into the state should store their firearms unloaded, locked in a secured case, and kept the trunk or rear compartment of a vehicle. To purchase a firearm in the state, residents must obtain a firearm identification card called a FOID card. The state's department of safety issues the card. The law also notes that certain instances of using a firearm for self-defense are justified. We highly advise anyone traveling into the state with a firearm to contact the state beforehand, as their laws are convoluted and highly restrictive. Guns are not allowed in the city of Chicago unless firearms are in transit as noted.

FIREARM FRIENDLY: F

*As of the summer of 2013, Illinois has voted to allow citizens to carry concealed handguns. The laws will adjust to this policy and make the state more gun friendly, as residents will be able to carry a concealed handgun.

Selective Excerpt From the State's Law:

Firearm Concealed Carry Act- Question and Answer from the Illinois State Police (ISP) concerning the state's shifting laws.

How will Illinois State Police (ISP) officers and local law enforcement respond to citizens who are carrying weapons?

The ISP will continue to enforce the law in effect. Citizens cannot lawfully carry concealed weapons without a valid Illinois Concealed Carry License. Citizens who carry firearms without a Concealed Carry License issued by the ISP are subject to arrest. All Illinois residents seeking to obtain a Concealed Carry License must have a valid Firearm Owner's Identification (FOID) card. Out-of-state residents are exempt from the FOID card requirement.

Who needs an Illinois Concealed Carry License?

Everyone who wants to carry a concealed firearm on his/her person in Illinois is required to have an Illinois Concealed Carry License except current peace officers and retired police officers eligible under the Illinois Retired Officer Concealed Carry (IROCC) Program. Retired officers may be eligible to carry under either the IROCC Program or the Firearm Concealed Carry Act (430 ILCS 66).

Are out-of-state Concealed Carry permit holders granted reciprocity in Illinois?

No. Out-of-state residents who want to carry a concealed firearm on his/her person must obtain an Illinois Concealed Carry License to lawfully carry a concealed firearm in Illinois. In order for out-of-state residents to be eligible for an Illinois license, their state's concealed carry license laws must be substantially similar to those of Illinois. The Illinois State Police will establish rules to identify the elements necessary to meet the substantially similar requirement. However, out of state residents are granted a limited exception to lawfully carry a concealed firearm within a vehicle if they are

Contact for Additional Information:
Illinois State Police
P.O. Box 19461 • Springfield, IL 62794-9461
217-281-5164

eligible to carry a firearm in public under the laws of his or her state or territory of residence and are not prohibited from owning or possessing a firearm under federal law. This rule becomes effective immediately. If the non-resident leaves his/her vehicle unattended, he or she shall store the firearm within a locked vehicle or locked container within the vehicle in accordance with subsection (b) of Section 65 of the Firearm Concealed Carry Act.

What is the cost for an Illinois Concealed Carry License?

$150 for 5 years for Illinois residents

$300 for 5 years for out-of-state residents

How does a citizen apply for an Illinois Concealed Carry License?

The ISP will make applications available to the public by January 5, 2014. The ISP intends to have applications available via the ISP webpage.

How long will it take a citizen to obtain an Illinois Concealed Carry license?

Upon receipt of a qualified application, the ISP shall issue or deny the applicant an Illinois Concealed Carry License within 90 days, provided the applicant submits a full set of fingerprints in electronic format. If fingerprints are not submitted in electronic format, the ISP is granted an additional 30 days to complete a manual background check. In all cases, law enforcement agencies will have 30 days to file and objection once an application is received.

Where can I go to be fingerprinted?

Concealed Carry License applicants are required to submit fingerprints for non-criminal justice purposes through a Licensed Illinois Livescan Vendor. A list of Licensed Livescan Vendors is available at the following link:

http://www.isp.state.il.us/docs/livescanfpvendlst.pdf

What is the penalty for carrying a weapon without a valid CCL?

Generally, an Unlawful Use of Weapons first offense is a Class A Misdemeanor and a second or subsequent offense is a Class 3 Felony; however, there are penalty enhancements for certain locations (for example on or within 1,000 feet of any school, public park, courthouse, public transportation facility, or residential public housing). Further, an Aggravated Unlawful Use of Weapons first offense is a Class 4 Felony and a second or subsequent offense is a Class 2 Felony.

FIREARM FRIENDLY: F

What are the qualifications for an Illinois Concealed Carry License?

The applicant must:

- Be at least 21 years of age

- Have a valid FOID card (if an Illinois resident)

- Have not been convicted or found guilty in Illinois or any other state of:

A misdemeanor involving the use or threat of physical force
or violence to any person within the last five years

Two or more violations related to driving while under the influence of
alcohol, other drug or drugs, intoxicating compound or compounds,
or any combination thereof, within the last five years

- Not be the subject of a pending arrest warrant, prosecution, or
proceeding for an offense or action that could lead to disqualification

- Not have been in residential or court-ordered treatment for alcoholism,
alcohol detoxification, or drug treatment within the last 5 years

- Submit a completed Concealed Carry License application

- Successfully complete 16 hours of firearms training,
including classroom and range instruction.

Is there a phone number I can call if I have questions
which are not addressed on this website?

Yes, however, you will only be able to leave a message regarding
your question, which will be addressed through an update to the
Frequently Asked Questions. Individual calls will not be returned.
Inquiries consistent with this may be directed to: (217) 782-7980.

**The historic Moore v. Madigan and
People v. Aguilar cases gave Illinois citizens
the right to carry concealed firearms.
Illinois became the last state to allow
residents to carry concealed weapons.**

IANA

Permit Carriers:

Concealed Carry: All citizens shall be issued a carry permit

Unconcealed Carry: All citizens shall be issued a carry permit

Traveling with a Firearm: May transport loaded handguns and long arms

Notifying Law Enforcement of Carry Permit and Firearm: Only required if requested by an officer.

Self-Defense Model: Castle doctrine. Stand your ground.

Restaurants: May carry firearms in restaurants that do not have posted signs noting otherwise and as long as alcohol is not consumed.

Recognizes Carry Permits Issued by: All states

Law Uniformity: Local agencies cannot make additional restrictions upon state law

All Citizens and Those Without Carry Permits:

Owning a Firearm: All citizens without license or permit

Owning a Semi-Auto: All citizens without license or permit

Owning a Machine Gun: All citizens without license or permit, must abide federal law

Carrying a Loaded Firearm in Public: Only when hunting and a person has a sporting license, otherwise it's forbidden.

Traveling with a Firearm: Loaded long arms can be transported if they're in plain view or in a gun case. Handguns should be unloaded, cased, and out of easy reach of passengers.

State Parks: Only permit carriers

Gun Possession on College Campuses: Determined by college administration

Additional Notes and Points of Interest: Indiana has fairly relaxed gun laws, but unconcealed or concealed carry of a weapon by a non-permit holder is not allowed unless the person is hunting and also has a sporting license.

Contact for Additional Information:
Indiana State Police
100 N. Senate Avenue/ IGCN • Indianapolis, IN 46204
317-232-8264

FIREARM FRIENDLY: A+

Selective Excerpt From the State's Law:

<u>IC 35-47-2 Regulation of Handguns IC 35-47-2-0.1 Carrying a handgun without being licensed; exceptions; person convicted of domestic battery</u>

Sec. 1. (a) Except as provided in subsections (b) and (c) and section 2 of this chapter, a person shall not carry a handgun in any vehicle or on or about the person's body without being licensed under this chapter to carry a handgun. (b) Except as provided in subsection (c), a person may carry a handgun without being licensed under this chapter to carry a handgun if:

(1) the person carries the handgun on or about the person's body in or on property that is owned, leased, rented, or otherwise legally controlled by the person;

(2) the person carries the handgun on or about the person's body while lawfully present in or on property that is owned, leased, rented, or otherwise legally controlled by another person, if the person: (A) has the consent of the owner, renter, less or, or person who legally controls the property to have the handgun on the premises; (B) is attending a firearms related event on the property, including a gun show, firearms expo, gun owner's club or convention, hunting club, shooting club, or training course; or (C) is on the property to receive firearms related services, including the repair, maintenance, or modification of a firearm;

(3) the person carries the handgun in a vehicle that is owned, leased, rented, or otherwise legally controlled by the person, if the handgun is: (A) unloaded; (B) not readily accessible; and (C) secured in a case;

(4) the person carries the handgun while lawfully present in a vehicle that is owned, leased, rented, or otherwise legally controlled by another person, if the handgun is: (A) unloaded; (B) not readily accessible; and (C) secured in a case; or

(5) the person carries the handgun: (A) at a shooting range (as defined in IC 14-22-31.5-3); (B) while attending a firearms instructional course; or (C) while engaged in a legal hunting activity.

(c) Unless the person's right to possess a firearm has been restored under IC 35-47-4-7, a person who has been convicted of domestic battery under IC 35-42-2-1.3 may not possess or carry a handgun.

IA

Permit Carriers:

Concealed Carry: All citizens shall be issued a carry permit

Unconcealed Carry: Yes, with permit

Traveling with a Firearm: All citizens with a carry permit may transport loaded handguns. Long arms should be transported unloaded.

Notifying Law Enforcement of Carry Permit and Firearm: Only required if requested by an officer.

Self-Defense Model: No castle doctrine. Duty to retreat.

Restaurants: May carry firearms in restaurants that do not have posted signs noting otherwise and as long as alcohol is not consumed.

Recognizes Carry Permits Issued by: All states

Law Uniformity: Local agencies cannot make additional restrictions upon state law

All Citizens and Those Without Carry Permits:

Owning a Firearm: All citizens without license or permit except for handguns

Owning a Semi-Auto: All citizens without license or permit

Owning a Machine Gun: Forbidden

Carrying a Loaded Firearm in Public: Only with permit

Traveling with Firearms: Firearms can be transported unloaded and stored in a secure case that cannot be hidden on a person or where the weapon remains inaccessible to passengers.

State Parks: Only permit carriers

Gun Possession on College Campuses: Not permitted

Additional Notes and Points of Interest: Regardless if an individual has his or her carry permit, firearms are not to be brought to casinos, fairs, state buildings, or carried on a snowmobile or similar ATC vehicle. All carbine rifles, machine guns, and short-barreled shotguns are illegal.

Contact for Additional Information:
Attorney General of Iowa
1305 E. Walnut, Hoover Bldg • Des Moines, IA 50319
515-281-5164

Selective Excerpt From the State's Law:

From the Frequently Asked Question Section on the State's Website

QUESTION: How long is my permit valid?

ANSWER: Nonprofessional permits to carry will be valid for five years from the date of issue (unless revoked). Professional permits to carry will remain valid for one year from the date of issuance (unless revoked).

QUESTION: Under the new law, do I have to carry my handgun concealed?

ANSWER: Iowa law has not changed in this regard. You may carry concealed or you may carry openly; however, most permit holders carry concealed to avoid making it obvious that the person is armed, thus avoiding unnecessary attention, concern, or alarm. Prepared by the Iowa Department of Public Safety Version 3.0, November 5, 2010 2

QUESTION: Can I carry other weapons besides my handgun?

ANSWER: Iowa law has not changed in this regard. An Iowa carry permit still allows for the concealed or open carrying of handguns, rifles, and shotguns, excluding those classified by Iowa law as offensive weapons (federal NFA or Class 3). An Iowa carry permit also allows the concealed carrying of other non-firearm dangerous weapons such as knives with blades in excess of five inches, switchblade knives, tasers/stun guns, or any other dangerous weapon. NOTE: Non-firearm dangerous weapons may be carried openly without a permit. Non-firearm dangerous weapons may also be regulated by local ordinance that is more stringent than Iowa law.

QUESTION: Does my Iowa permit to carry allow me to have a loaded firearm anywhere in my vehicle?

ANSWER: Yes. You may carry a loaded handgun, rifle or shotgun in a motor vehicle; however this does not apply to snowmobiles or all-terrain vehicles (see Iowa Department of Natural Resources: Iowa Hunting Laws and Weapons Permit Applicability)

QUESTION: Does an Iowa permit to carry allow me to carry a firearm during certain restricted hunting seasons or while in state parks?

ANSWER: Check the following link to the Iowa Department of Natural Resources: Iowa Hunting Laws and Weapons Permit Applicability

QUESTION: If I am stopped by a law enforcement officer in Iowa, am I required to declare that I am carrying a loaded firearm?

ANSWER: No, but it is really good idea. Iowa law does not require such a declaration; however, as a safety measure for both the permit holder and the officer, making such a declaration voluntarily is recommended and encouraged.

QUESTION: Will my Iowa driver's license be flagged to indicate that I have an Iowa permit to carry?

ANSWER: No. Iowa law does not provide for this.

QUESTION: Can fingerprints be collected in conjunction with submittal of an application for a permit?

ANSWER: If an issuing officer encounters a situation that involves a dispute related to the identity of an applicant or a conviction that is attributed to an applicant, the submission of fingerprints may be the most expedient method to clear up the dispute regarding identity or criminal history. Fingerprints might also help to accelerate the process of an appeal to the FBI of a denial based on a NICS check.

KANSAS

Permit Carriers:

Concealed Carry: All citizens shall be issued a carry permit

Unconcealed Carry: Unrestricted but local agencies may regulate use

Traveling with a Firearm: May travel with a handgun on one's person

Notifying Law Enforcement of Carry Permit and Firearm: Only required if requested by an officer.

Self-Defense Model: Castle doctrine. Stand your ground in public.

Restaurants: May carry firearms in restaurants that do not have posted signs noting otherwise and as long as alcohol is not consumed.

Recognizes Carry Permits Issued by: Alaska, Arizona, Arkansas, Colorado, Florida, Hawaii, Kentucky, Louisiana, Michigan, Minnesota, Missouri, Nebraska, Nevada, New Jersey, New Mexico, North Carolina, North Dakota, Ohio, Oklahoma, South Carolina, Tennessee, Texas, West Virginia

Law Uniformity: Local laws may differ

All Citizens and Those Without Carry Permits:

Owning a Firearm: All citizens without license or permit

Owning a Semi-Auto: All citizens without license or permit

Owning a Machine Gun: All citizens without license or permit, must abide federal law

Carrying a Loaded Firearm in Public: Largely Forbidden. Non-permit carriers may have handguns while hunting.

Traveling with Firearms: While laws in the state differ, long arms should be cased and unloaded when transported. Most cities also allow non-permit carriers to travel with a loaded handgun as long as it remains in plain view and is not concealed on the person.

State Parks: Only permit carriers

Gun Possession on College Campuses: Only permit carriers

Additional Notes and Points of Interest: Keeping track of the laws in Kansas may prove difficult as they differ from location to location, but a permit carrier would remain within the confines of the law if all firearms are cased and unloaded during transport. Additionally, if a permit carrier resides or is passing through the state, he or she should check with the local or state government to determine what additional restrictions may be applied to state law.

Contact for Additional Information:
Attorney General of Kansas
120 SW Tenth Ave-2nd Floor • Topeka, KS 66612-1597
785-291-3765

FIREARM FRIENDLY: A

Selective Excerpt From the State's Law:

Frequently Asked Questions Listed on the State's Website:

QUESTION: What does the amendment in Section 1 do?

ANSWER: This amendment addresses K.S.A. 12-16,124(a) and 12-16,124(d) by cleaning up a reference in each to an old KPFPA statute (75-7c11) that was repealed in 2010. It also amends 12-16,124(b)(2) and (b)(4) so that those protections are afforded to CCLs (concealed carry license) from other jurisdictions which are recognized by Kansas.1

QUESTION: I have an expunged felony conviction. Do the changes in Sections 2 and 3 of SB 21 mean that that expunged conviction cannot be used when reviewing my application?

ANSWER: Generally, no. Prior felony convictions that occur in Kansas' state court system result in four (4) categories of firearm prohibition periods in Kansas: lifetime (under subsection (a)(1)); a 10 year prohibition for more serious person and drug felonies (under (a)(3)(A)) or for certain nonperson felonies (under (a)(3)(B)); and a catch-all 5 year prohibition period under (a)(2) for any felony that does not fit subsections (a)(1) or (a)(3).2. Under Kansas law, the general rule is that the expungement of a felony conviction will not sever any state or federal firearms prohibition. The amendment in Section 2 to K.S.A. 21-6304 and the amendments to K.S.A. 21-6614 in Section 3 reiterate this point. They make it clear that the only time a firearms prohibition is severed by expungement (or pardon) of a prior felony is when that prior felony conviction falls into 21-6304(a)(3)(A). NOTE: The expungement of that felony will only sever any firearm's restrictions for that felony; if the individual has other criminal history that resulted in a loss of firearm rights then that loss is not affected by the expungement. Some felony offenses listed in (a)(3)(A) are not expungeable, however. If you have felony criminal history, you need to consult with private legal counsel about your specific situation and discuss whether Kansas law allows you to possess firearms. Felony convictions that occurred in another state or in any federal court will have to survive the firearms expungement, set-aside, pardon or restoration procedures of that other jurisdiction and the restoration procedures of Kansas law under 21-6304 before the individual will be considered eligible to possess firearms in Kansas (and, therefore, be eligible for a CCL).

QUESTION: I live in another state and have a non-expired CCL from that State. Am I lawful to carry concealed handguns in Kansas?

ANSWER: On and after July 1, 2013, Kansas will honor any "valid" concealed carry license that is issued by another state or the District of Columbia so long as the holder of that CCL is not a resident of Kansas. Section 4 of SB 21 amends K.S.A. 75-7c03 to allow this broader recognition. So long as the non-Kansas CCL is "valid" (defined as non-expired and not revoked or suspended) and so long as the holder is not a resident of Kansas, that non-Kansas CCL will be honored by Kansas.

Permit Carriers:

Concealed Carry: All citizens shall be issued a carry permit

Unconcealed Carry: Yes, all citizens

Traveling with a Firearm: May transport loaded handguns and long arms

Notifying Law Enforcement of Carry Permit and Firearm: Only required if requested by an officer.

Self-Defense Model: Castle doctrine. Stand your ground.

Restaurants: May carry firearms in restaurants that do not have posted signs noting otherwise and as long as alcohol is not consumed.

Recognizes Carry Permits Issued by: All states

Law Uniformity: Local agencies cannot make additional restrictions upon state law

All Citizens and Those Without Carry Permits:

Owning a Firearm: All citizens without license or permit

Owning a Semi-Auto: All citizens without license or permit

Owning a Machine Gun: All citizens without license or permit, must abide federal law

Carrying a Loaded Firearm in Public: Travelers may carry holstered handguns in public without a permit

Traveling with a Firearm: Loaded firearms can be transported if they remain in plain view, whether being on a belt holster, dashboard, or in the passenger's seat. Long arms should be secured in gun racks or cases. Unloaded firearms can be stored around the vehicle.

State Parks: Only permit carriers

Gun Possession on College Campuses: Forbidden

Additional Notes and Points of Interest: Guns are not allowed at colleges, hospitals, bars, businesses with posted signs, the Kentucky State Fair, and state buildings.

Contact for Additional Information:
Kentucky State Police
919 Versailles Road • Frankfort, KY 40601
502-782-1800

FIREARM FRIENDLY: A+

Selective Excerpt From the State's Law:

<u>Concealed Deadly Weapon Qualifications as Mandated By State Police:</u>

The applicant for a carry concealed deadly weapon (CCDW) license must:

1. Meet one of the following residence requirements:

Is a citizen of the United States who is a resident of Kentucky and has been a resident for six (6) months or longer immediately preceding the filing of the application;

Is a citizen of the United States who is a member of the Armed Forces of the United States who is on active duty, who is at the time of application assigned to a military posting in Kentucky, and who has been assigned to a posting in the Commonwealth for six (6) months or longer immediately preceding the filing of the application; Is lawfully admitted to the United States by the United States government or an agency thereof, is permitted by federal law to purchase a firearm, and has been a resident of this Commonwealth for six (6) months or longer immediately preceding the filing of the application; or Is lawfully admitted to the United States by the United States government or an agency thereof, is permitted by federal law to purchase a firearm, is, at the time of the application, assigned to a military posting in Kentucky, and has been assigned to a posting in the Commonwealth for six (6) months or longer immediately preceding the filing of the application

2. Not be under indictment for, or have been convicted of, a crime punishable by imprisonment for a term exceeding one year; and

3. Not have been adjudicated as a mental defective or have committed to a mental institution; and

4. Not have been discharged from the Armed Forces under dishonorable conditions; and

5. Not be subject to a domestic violence order or emergency protective order; and

6. Not have been convicted of a misdemeanor crime of domestic violence (see section below for discussion of misdemeanor crimes of domestic violence); and

7. Not be prohibited from the purchase, receipt or possession of firearms, ammunition or both pursuant to 18 U.S.C. 922(g), 18 U.S.C. 922(n), or applicable state law; and

8. Not have been committed to a state or federal facility for abuse of a controlled substance or convicted of a misdemeanor relating to a controlled substance within the three-year period immediately preceding the date the application was submitted; and

9. Not have two or more convictions for violating KRS 189A.010 (Operating motor vehicle under the influence of alcohol or other substance which impairs driving ability) within the three (3) years immediately preceding the date on which the application is submitted; and

10. Not have been committed as an alcoholic pursuant to KRS Chapter 222 or similar laws of another state within the three (3) year period immediately preceding the date on which the application is submitted; and

11. Demonstrate competence with a firearm by successful completion of a firearms safety or training course offered or approved by the Department of Criminal Justice Training.

Permit Carriers:

Concealed Carry: All citizens shall be issued a carry permit.

Unconcealed Carry: Largely unrestricted for any persons (even though without a permit) to carry a handgun in public as long as the gun remains in plain view on a belt holster

Traveling with a Firearm: May transport loaded handguns. It's advisable that long arms be transported unloaded and cased, as the law remains vague.

Notifying Law Enforcement of Carry Permit and Firearm: Immediately upon making contact with an officer.

Self-Defense Model: Castle doctrine. Stand your ground.

Restaurants: No firearms can be brought in establishments that serve alcohol

Recognizes Carry Permits Issued by: Alabama, Alaska, Arizona, Arkansas, Colorado, Florida, Georgia, Idaho, Indiana, Iowa, Kansas, Kentucky, Maine, Michigan, Minnesota, Mississippi, Missouri, Montana, Nebraska, Nevada, New Hampshire, North Carolina, North Dakota, Ohio, Oklahoma, Pennsylvania, South Carolina, South Dakota, Tennessee, Texas, Utah, Virginia, Washington, West Virginia, Wisconsin, Wyoming

Law Uniformity: Some local agencies have differing laws that existed before 1985

All Citizens and Those Without Carry Permits:

Owning a Firearm: All citizens without license or permit

Owning a Semi-Auto: All citizens without license or permit

Owning a Machine Gun: Only historic war relics permitted, most machine guns forbidden

Carrying a Loaded Firearm in Public: Largely unrestricted for any persons to carry a handgun in public as long as the gun remains in plain view on a snapped belt holster

Traveling with a Firearm: Loaded handguns may be transported in plain view or in a glove box, console, trunk, or rear compartment of a vehicle. Long arms should be transported unloaded and stored in cases or gun racks.

State Parks: Only permit carriers

Gun Possession on College Campuses: Forbidden

Additional Notes and Points of Interest: The State forbids guns to be brought where they are normally banned in other states, such as state buildings, schools, parades, and college campuses. Businesses are also forbidden to deny patrons and employees from storing firearms in their vehicles, so traveling with a firearm through the state should be easy and of no conflict.

FIREARM FRIENDLY: A+

Selective Excerpt From the State's Law:

A. To qualify for a concealed handgun permit, a Louisiana resident shall:

(1) Make sworn application to the deputy secretary of public safety services of the Department of Public Safety and Corrections. The providing of false or misleading information on the application or any documents submitted with the application shall be grounds for the denial or revocation of a concealed handgun permit. The application shall reflect training in pistols, revolvers, or both. Any permittee under this Section shall notify the department of any address or name change within thirty days of the change. Failure to timely notify the department of a name or address change may result in suspension of the permit for up to thirty days.

(2) Agree in writing to hold harmless and indemnify the department, the state, or any peace officer for any and all liability arising out of the issuance or use of the concealed handgun permit.

(3) Be a resident of the state.

(4) Be twenty-one years of age or older.

(5) Not suffer from a mental or physical infirmity due to disease, illness, or retardation which prevents the safe handling of a handgun.

(6) Not be ineligible to possess a firearm by virtue of having been convicted of a felony.

(7) Not have been committed, either voluntarily or involuntarily, for the abuse of a controlled dangerous substance, as defined by R.S. 40:961 and 964, or been found guilty of, or entered a plea of guilty or nolo contendere to a misdemeanor under the laws of this state or similar laws of any other state relating to a controlled dangerous substance within a five-year period immediately preceding the date on which the application is submitted, or be presently charged under indictment or a bill of information for such an offense.

(8) Not chronically and habitually use alcoholic beverages to the extent that his normal faculties are impaired.

(9) Not be an unlawful user of, or addicted to, marijuana, depressants, stimulants, or narcotic drugs.

(10) Not have been adjudicated to be mentally deficient or been committed to a mental institution.

(11) Not have been discharged from the Armed Forces of the United States with a discharge characterized as "Under Other than Honorable Conditions", a "Bad Conduct Discharge", or a "Dishonorable Discharge".

LOUISIANA

Contact for Additional Information:
Louisiana State Police/ CHP Section
P.O. Box 66375 • Baton Rouge, LA 70896-6375
225-925-4867

Permit Carriers:

Concealed Carry: All citizens shall be issued a carry permit

Unconcealed Carry: Largely unrestricted for any individual (even those without a permit) to carry a handgun in public as long as the gun remains in plain view on a belt holster, but permit carriers should use extreme discretion when doing so.

Traveling with a Firearm: Loaded handguns may be transported on a person, but long arms should be transported unloaded

Notifying Law Enforcement of Carry Permit and Firearm: Only required if requested by an officer.

Self-Defense Model: No castle doctrine. Duty to retreat in public.

Restaurants: Forbidden in restaurants serving alcohol

Recognizes Carry Permits Issued by: Arkansas, Delaware, Louisiana, Michigan, North Dakota, Pennsylvania, South Dakota, Wyoming

Law Uniformity: Local agencies cannot make additional restrictions to most aspects of the state's gun law.

All Citizens and Those Without Carry Permits:

Owning a Firearm: All citizens without license or permit

Owning a Semi-Auto: All citizens without license or permit

Owning a Machine Gun: All citizens without license or permit must abide federal law

Carrying a Loaded Firearm in Public: Largely unrestricted for any individual to carry a handgun in public as long as the gun remains in plain view on a belt holster, but permit carriers should use extreme discretion for doing so. Hunters can legally carry a concealed weapon as long as they are actively hunting.

Traveling with Firearms: Unloaded handguns may be transported as long as they remain in plain view. They may also be transported if they are unloaded, cased, and stored in a trunk or rear compartment. No loaded firearms should be transported.

State Parks: Only permit carriers

Gun Possession on College Campuses: Dependent on college administration

Additional Notes and Points of Interest: While Maine is fairly firearm friendly, still use discretion when traveling through the state and ensure long arms and handguns remain unloaded if the state does not recognize ones carry permit. The state prohibits firearms from normal locations, such as state buildings, schools, and parades. State employees may keep firearms locked in their vehicles while on state property.

FIREARM FRIENDLY: A

MAINE

Selective Excerpt From the State's Law:

Maine's Laws Relating to Permits to Carry Concealed Firearms.

25 M.R.S.A. § 2001-A. Threatening display of or carrying concealed weapon

1. Display or carrying prohibited. A person may not, unless excepted by aprovision of law: A. Display in a threatening manner a firearm, slungshot, knuckles, bowie knife, dirk, stiletto or other dangerous or deadly weapon usually employed in the attack on or defense of a person; or B. Wear under the person's clothes or conceal about the person's person a firearm, slungshot, knuckles, bowie knife, dirk, stiletto or other dangerous or deadly weapon usually employed in the attack on or defense of a person.

2. Exceptions. The provisions of this section concerning the carrying of concealed weapons do not apply to: A. Firearms carried by a person to whom a valid permit to carry a concealed firearm has been issued as provided in this chapter; B. Disabling chemicals as described in Title 17-A, section 1002; C. Knives used to hunt, fish or trap as defined in Title 12, section 10001; D. Law enforcement officers and corrections officers as permitted in writing by their employer; E. Firearms carried by a person engaged in conduct for which a state-issued hunting or trapping license is required and possessing the required license, or firearms carried by a resident person engaged in conduct expressly authorized by Title 12, section 11108 and section 12202, subsection 1.1 This paragraph does not authorize or permit the carrying of a concealed or loaded firearm in a motor vehicle; and F. A firearm carried by a person to whom a valid permit to carry a concealed firearm has been issued by another state if a permit to carry a concealed firearm issued from that state has been granted reciprocity. The Chief of the State Police may enter into reciprocity agreements with 2 other states. Reciprocity may be granted to a permit to carry a concealed firearm issued from another state if: (1) The other state that issued the permit to carry a concealed firearm has substantially equivalent or stricter requirements for the issuance of a permit to carry a concealed firearm; and (2) The other state that issued the permit to carry a concealed firearm observes the same rules of reciprocity in regards to a person issued a permit to carry a concealed firearm under this chapter.

Contact for Additional Information:
Maine Department of Public Safety
45 Commerce/ State House 164 • Augusta, ME 04333
207-624-7210

Permit Carriers:

Concealed Carry: Permitted, but issued with discretion

Unconcealed Carry: Allowed if one has a carry permit

Traveling with a Firearm: Permitted. Long arms should be transported unloaded and stored in a case or gun rack.

Notifying Law Enforcement of Carry Permit and Firearm: Only required if requested by an officer.

Self-Defense Model: No castle doctrine, duty to retreat in public.

Restaurants: May carry firearms in restaurants that do not have posted signs noting otherwise and as long as alcohol is not consumed.

Recognizes Carry Permits Issued by: No states

Law Uniformity: Local agencies cannot make additional restrictions upon state law

All Citizens and Those Without Carry Permits:

Owning a Firearm: All citizens without license or permit

Owning a Semi-Auto: All citizens without license or permit

Owning a Machine Gun: All citizens without license or permit, must abide federal law

Carrying a Loaded Firearm in Public: Forbidden without permit

Traveling with Firearms: A firearm cannot be transported loaded or easily accessible to passengers. Unloaded handguns can be transported to legitimate firearm events, such as licensed gun shows, shooting ranges, and hunting locations. Visitors may travel with unloaded handguns if they are passing through the state. All firearms should be cased, unloaded, and stored a trunks or rear storage compartments or locked in a case if a vehicle lacks a trunk.

State Parks: Forbidden

Gun Possession on College Campuses: Dependent on college administration

Additional Notes and Points of Interest: New laws now legally protect homeowners who use deadly force against home intruders. Firearms cannot be brought within 100 yards of public parks, churches, public facilities, and places of assembly.

Selective Excerpt From the State's Law:

<u>Frequently Asked Questions from the State Police's Website.</u>

QUESTION: How can I legally transport firearms within / through Maryland?

ANSWER: They must be unloaded, in a carrying case, holster with a flap and the ammunition should be separate. It would be best to keep the unloaded weapon in the trunk where you do not have access to it. There are further regulations but essentially you can only transport a handgun between residence, to and from a repair shop, a shooting sporting event, between a residence and place of business if substantially owned and operated by the person. For more information please contact our Licensing Division.

QUESTION: How do you become a gunsmith, retail or wholesale firearms dealer, or get information on ammunition sales and/or gunsmithing?

ANSWER: Please contact our Licensing Division for that information.

QUESTION: Is it legal for me to carry a concealed weapon in Maryland?

ANSWER: Only with a permit that you must apply for through the Licensing Division.

QUESTION: How can I legally transport firearms within / through Maryland?

ANSWER: They must be unloaded, in a carrying case, holster with a flap and the ammunition should be separate. It would be best to keep the unloaded weapon in the trunk where you do not have access to it. There are further regulations but essentially you can only transport a handgun between residence, to and from a repair shop, a shooting sporting event, between a residence and place of business if substantially owned and operated by the person. For more information please contact our Licensing Division.

MARYLAND

Contact for Additional Information:
Attorney General of Maryland
200 Saint Paul Place • Baltimore, MD 21202
410-576-6300

Permit Carriers:

Concealed Carry: Yes, but issued with discretion

Unconcealed Carry: Yes, but only with carry permit

Traveling with a Firearm: Individuals with a carry permit may travel with a handgun in their control and out of reach of others.

Notifying Law Enforcement of Carry Permit and Firearm: Only required if requested by an officer

Self-Defense Model: No castle doctrine. Duty to retreat in public

Restaurants: Permit carriers can carry firearms in restaurants that do not have posted signs noting otherwise and as long as alcohol is not consumed.

Recognizes Carry Permits Issued by: The state doesn't disclose what other states carry permits they accept, but one with a carry permit traveling into the state must strictly follow the state's laws concerning firearms. Because of the ambiguity of their laws, it's not advised that individuals from out of state carry a loaded, uncased firearm into the state.

Law Uniformity: Laws are uniformly anti-gun across the state

All Citizens and Those Without Carry Permits:

Owning a Firearm: Need license to purchase

Owning a Semi-Auto: Need license to purchase. No assault rifle produced after 1994 allowed.

Owning a Machine Gun: Heavily restricted, one must get a purchasing permit and abide by federal law

Carrying a Loaded Firearm in Public: Forbidden

Traveling with Handguns: Transporting an unloaded handgun is largely forbidden unless a person is passing through the state. Shotguns and rifles may be transported as long as they remain unloaded and secured in a case.

State Parks: Only permit carriers

Gun Possession on College Campuses: Forbidden

Additional Notes and Points of Interest: The state has very strict gun laws, as carry permits are issued only on extremely discretionary basis. Individuals should use extreme discretion before transporting a firearm in the state and ensure the gun is unloaded and secured in a case. Non-residents and visitors may be granted temporary carry permits if they already have a carry permit from another state and visitors can also use and transport firearms for hunting purposes. It is recommended individuals contact the Firearms Bureau of Massachusetts if they have any additional questions about bringing weapons into the state.

MASSACHUSETTS

Selective Excerpt From the State's Law:

License firearms Class A and B; conditions and restrictions

Section 131. All licenses to carry firearms shall be designated Class A or Class B, and the issuance and possession of any such license shall be subject to the following conditions and restrictions:

(a) A Class A license shall entitle a holder thereof to purchase, rent, lease, borrow, possess and carry: (i) firearms, including large capacity firearms, and feeding devices and ammunition therefore, for all lawful purposes, subject to such restrictions relative to the possession, use or carrying of firearms as the licensing authority deems proper; and (ii) rifles and shotguns, including large capacity weapons, and feeding devices and ammunition therefore, for all lawful purposes; provided, however, that the licensing authority may impose such restrictions relative to the possession, use or carrying of large capacity rifles and shotguns as it deems proper. A violation of a restriction imposed by the licensing authority under the provisions of this paragraph shall be cause for suspension or revocation and shall, unless otherwise provided, be punished by a fine of not less than $1,000 nor more than $10,000; provided, however, that the provisions of section 10 of chapter 269 shall not apply to such violation.

The colonel of state police may, after an investigation, grant a Class A license to a club or facility with an on-site shooting range or gallery, which club is incorporated under the laws of the commonwealth for the possession, storage and use of large capacity weapons, ammunition therefore and large capacity feeding devices for use with such weapons on the premises of such club; provided, however, that not less than one shareholder of such club shall be qualified and suitable to be issued such license; and provided further, that such large capacity weapons and ammunition feeding devices may be used under such Class A club license only by such members who possess a valid firearm identification card issued under section 129B or a valid Class A or Class B license to carry firearms, or by such other persons that the club permits while under the direct supervision of a certified firearms safety instructor or club member who, in the case of a large capacity firearm, possesses a valid Class A license to carry firearms or, in the case of a large capacity rifle or shotgun, possesses a valid Class A or Class B license to carry firearms. Such club shall not permit shooting at targets that depict human figures, human effigies, human silhouettes or any human images thereof, except by public safety personnel performing in line with their official duties.

Contact for Additional Information:
Firearms Bureau of Massachusetts
200 Arlington Street, Ste. 220 • Chelsea, MA 02150
617-660-4780

No large capacity weapon or large capacity feeding device shall be removed from the premises except for the purposes of: (i) transferring such firearm or feeding device to a licensed dealer; (ii) transporting such firearm or feeding device to a licensed gunsmith for repair; (iii) target, trap or skeet shooting on the premises of another club incorporated under the laws of the commonwealth and for transporting thereto; (iv) attending an exhibition or educational project or event that is sponsored by, conducted under the supervision of or approved by a public law enforcement agency or a nationally or state recognized entity that promotes proficiency in or education about semiautomatic weapons and for transporting thereto and therefrom; (v) hunting in accordance with the provisions of chapter 131; or (vi) surrendering such firearm or feeding device under the provisions of section 129D. Any large capacity weapon or large capacity feeding device kept on the premises of a lawfully incorporated shooting club shall, when not in use, be secured in a locked container, and shall be unloaded during any lawful transport. The clerk or other corporate officer of such club shall annually file a report with the colonel of state police and the commissioner of the department of criminal justice information services listing all large capacity weapons and large capacity feeding devices owned or possessed under such license. The colonel of state police or his designee, shall have the right to inspect all firearms owned or possessed by such club upon request during regular business hours and said colonel may revoke or suspend a club license for a violation of any provision of this chapter or chapter 269 relative to the ownership, use or possession of large capacity weapons or large capacity feeding devices.

(b) A Class B license shall entitle a holder thereof to purchase, rent, lease, borrow, possess and carry: (i) non-large capacity firearms and feeding devices and ammunition therefore, for all lawful purposes, subject to such restrictions relative to the possession, use or carrying of such firearm as the licensing authority deems proper; provided, however, that a Class B license shall not entitle the holder thereof to carry or possess a loaded firearm in a concealed manner in any public way or place; and provided further, that a Class B license shall not entitle the holder thereof to possess a large capacity firearm, except under a Class A club license issued under this section or under the direct supervision of a holder of a valid Class A license at an incorporated shooting club or licensed shooting range; and (ii) rifles and shotguns, including large capacity rifles and shotguns, and feeding devices and ammunition therefore, for all lawful purposes; provided, however, that the licensing authority may impose such restrictions relative to the possession, use or carrying of large capacity rifles and shotguns as he or she deems proper. A violation of a restriction provided under this paragraph, or a restriction imposed by the licensing authority under the provisions of this paragraph, shall be cause for suspension or revocation and shall, unless otherwise provided, be punished by a fine of not less than $1,000 nor more than $10,000; provided, however, that the provisions of section 10 of chapter 269 shall not apply to such violation.

A Class B license shall not be a valid license for the purpose of complying with any provision under this chapter governing the purchase, sale, lease, rental or transfer of any weapon or ammunition feeding device if such weapon is a large capacity firearm or if such ammunition feeding device is a large capacity feeding device for use with a large capacity firearm, both as defined in section 121.

(c) Either a Class A or Class B license shall be valid for the purpose of owning, possessing, purchasing and transferring non-large capacity rifles and shotguns, and for purchasing and possessing chemical mace, pepper spray or other similarly propelled liquid, gas or powder designed to temporarily incapacitate, consistent with the entitlements conferred by a firearm identification card issued under section 129B.

(d) Any person residing or having a place of business within the jurisdiction of the licensing authority or any law enforcement officer employed by the licensing authority or any person residing in an area of exclusive federal jurisdiction located within a city or town may submit to such licensing authority or the colonel of state police, an application for a Class A or Class B license to carry firearms, or renewal of the same, which such licensing authority or said colonel may issue if it appears that the applicant is a suitable person to be issued such license, and that the applicant has good reason to fear injury to his person or property, or for any other reason, including the carrying of firearms for use in sport or target practice only, subject to such restrictions expressed or authorized under this section, unless the applicant:

(i) has, in any state or federal jurisdiction, been convicted or adjudicated a youthful offender or delinquent child for the commission of (a) a felony; (b) a misdemeanor punishable by imprisonment for more than two years; (c) a violent crime as defined in section 121; (d) a violation of any law regulating the use, possession, ownership, transfer, purchase, sale, lease, rental, receipt or transportation of weapons or ammunition for which a term of imprisonment may be imposed; or (e) a violation of any law regulating the use, possession or sale of controlled substances as defined in section 1 of chapter 94C;

(ii) has been confined to any hospital or institution for mental illness, unless the applicant submits with his application an affidavit of a registered physician attesting that such physician is familiar with the applicant's mental illness and that in such physician's opinion the applicant is not disabled by such an illness in a manner that should prevent such applicant from possessing a firearm;

(iii) is or has been under treatment for or confinement for drug addiction or habitual drunkenness, unless such applicant is deemed to be cured of such condition by a licensed physician, and such applicant may make application for such license after the expiration of five years from the date of such confinement or treatment and upon presentment of an affidavit issued by such physician stating that such physician knows the applicant's history of treatment and that in such physician's opinion the applicant is deemed cured;

(iv) is at the time of the application less than 21 years of age;

(v) is an alien;

(vi) is currently subject to: (A) an order for suspension or surrender issued pursuant to section 3B or 3C of chapter 209A or a similar order issued by another jurisdiction; or (B) a permanent or temporary protection order issued pursuant to chapter 209A or a similar order issued by another jurisdiction; or

(vii) is currently the subject of an outstanding arrest warrant in any state or federal jurisdiction.

MASSACHUSETTS

Permit Carriers:

Concealed Carry: All citizens shall be issued a carry permit

Unconcealed Carry: Unrestricted, but not advised or normal in the state

Traveling with a Firearm: May carry a concealed handgun with carry permit

Notifying Law Enforcement of Carry Permit and Firearm:
Immediately upon making contact with an officer.

Self-Defense Model: Castle doctrine. Stand your ground.

Restaurants: May carry firearms in restaurants that do not have
posted signs noting otherwise and as long as alcohol is not consumed.

Recognizes Carry Permits Issued by: All states

Law Uniformity: Local agencies cannot make
additional restrictions upon state law

All Citizens and Those Without Carry Permits:

Owning a Firearm: Unrestricted unless buying
a handgun, which requires a license.

Owning a Semi-Auto: Permitted with limited exceptions,
including certain models of carbine rifles

Owning a Machine Gun: All citizens without license
or permit, but must abide federal law

Carrying a Loaded Firearm in Public: Handguns can
be carried unconcealed, but this is not advised. Individuals
must have a carry permit to carry a concealed weapon.

Traveling with Firearms: Long arms must be transported
unloaded or either secured in a case, disassembled, or
placed in a trunk and inaccessible by passengers.

State Parks: Only permit carriers

Gun Possession on College Campuses: Only permit carriers, except at
Wayne State University and The University of Michigan, which forbid firearms.

Additional Notes and Points of Interest: Though much of the
state is fairly rural, Michigan has surprisingly strict gun laws. When
transporting pistols, Michigan residents without their carry permit should
ensure they're heading to or from locations where handguns are legally
permitted, like shooting ranges and sanctioned gun shows. It is legally
impossible to transport a handgun into the state unless a person has a
carry permit from his or her home state. Also note that while non-permit
carriers can carry unconcealed handguns in public, they cannot do so in
their vehicles and must unload and secure their handgun before driving.

FIREARM FRIENDLY: B

Selective Excerpt From the State's Law:

<u>State of Michigan Enrolled House Bill No. 5225</u>

AN ACT to amend 1927 PA 372, entitled "An act to regulate and license the selling, purchasing, possessing, and carrying of certain firearms, gas ejecting devices, and electro-muscular disruption devices; to prohibit the buying, selling, or carrying of certain firearms, gas ejecting devices, and electro-muscular disruption devices without a license or other authorization; to provide for the forfeiture of firearms and electro-muscular disruption devices under certain circumstances; to provide for penalties and remedies; to provide immunity from civil liability under certain circumstances; to prescribe the powers and duties of certain state and local agencies; to prohibit certain conduct against individuals who apply for or receive a license to carry a concealed pistol; to make appropriations; to prescribe certain conditions for the appropriations; and to repeal all acts and parts of acts inconsistent with this act," by amending sections 2 and 2a (MCL 28.422 and 28.422a), section 2 as amended by 2010 PA 20 and section 2a as amended by 2010 PA 210; and to repeal acts and parts of acts.

The People of the State of Michigan enact:

Sec. 2. (1) Except as otherwise provided in this act, a person shall not purchase, carry, possess, or transport a pistol in this state without first having obtained a license for the pistol as prescribed in this section.

(2) A person who brings a pistol into this state who is on leave from active duty with the armed forces of the United States or who has been discharged from active duty with the armed forces of the United States shall obtain a license for the pistol within 30 days after his or her arrival in this state.

(3) The commissioner or chief of police of a city, township, or village police department that issues licenses to purchase, carry, possess, or transport pistols, or his or her duly authorized deputy, or the sheriff or his or her duly authorized deputy, in the parts of a county not included within a city, township, or village having an organized police department, in discharging the duty to issue licenses shall with due speed and diligence issue licenses to purchase, carry, possess, or transport pistols to qualified applicants unless he or she has probable cause to believe that the applicant would be a threat to himself or herself or to other individuals, or would commit an offense with the pistol that would violate a law of this or another state or of the United States.

Contact for Additional Information:
Michigan State Police
P.O. Box 30634 • Lansing, MI 48909
517-332-2521

MINNESOTA

Permit Carriers:

Concealed Carry: All citizens shall be issued a carry permit.

Unconcealed Carry: Yes, permit carriers can carry.

Traveling with a Firearm: May carry a concealed handgun with a carry permit. Long arms should be unloaded and stored in a case or trunk.

Notifying Law Enforcement of Carry Permit and Firearm: Only required if requested by an officer.

Self-Defense Model: No castle doctrine. Duty to retreat.

Restaurants: May carry firearms in restaurants that do not have posted signs noting otherwise and as long as alcohol is not consumed.

Recognizes Carry Permits Issued by: Alaska, Arkansas, Kansas, Kentucky, Louisiana, Michigan, Missouri, Nevada, New Mexico, Ohio, Oklahoma, Tennessee, Texas, Utah, Wyoming

Law Uniformity: Local agencies cannot make additional restrictions upon state law

All Citizens and Those Without Carry Permits:

Owning a Firearm: Unrestricted unless buying a handgun, which requires a license.

Owning a Semi-Auto: All citizens without license or permit

Owning a Machine Gun: Largely forbidden, only replicas or curios may be owned

Carrying a Loaded Firearm in Public: Forbidden unless with carry permit

Traveling with Firearms: Handguns must be unloaded and cased but can be stored in the passenger compartment. The same applies to long arms. Long arms can be stored unloaded in a trunk or rear compartment without a case.

State Parks: Permit carriers may carry concealed weapons.

Gun Possession on College Campuses: Forbidden

Additional Notes and Points of Interest: Hunters and sport shooters may carry handguns while actively hunting or shooting without a permit. A person can also briefly transport their firearm from his or her vehicle to home or work place without a permit. Long arms should only be carried loaded while hunting.

Contact for Additional Information:
Minnesota Dept. of Public Safety
445 Minnesota St. • St. Paul, MN 55101
651-215-1328

FIREARM FRIENDLY: A

Selective Excerpt From the State's Law:

Frequently Asked Questions Provided by the State's Bureau
of Criminal Apprehension.

These answers are for information purposes only. Further clarification of the law may be addressed by referring directly to Minnesota State Statute 624.714.

QUESTION: Where can I apply for a permit to carry a pistol?

ANSWER: For Minnesota residents, individuals may obtain permits to carry a pistol by submitting an application and other related documentation to the sheriff in the county where the applicant resides. Non-residents may apply to any Minnesota county sheriff.

QUESTION: What are the requirements for getting a permit to carry?

ANSWER: Must be at least 21 years of age

Must complete an application form

Must not be prohibited from possessing a firearm under Minnesota Statute 624.714

Must not be listed in the criminal gang investigation system

Must be a resident of the county from which you are requesting a permit, if you reside in Minnesota. Non-residents may apply to any Minnesota county sheriff.

Must provide certificate of completed authorized firearms training. Training by a certified instructor must be completed within one year of an original or renewal application. (624.714, Subd. 2a)

QUESTION: How long is my permit valid?

ANSWER: New and renewal permits are valid for five (5) years from the date of issuance. Emergency permits are valid for 30 days.

QUESTION: What would prevent me from getting a permit to carry?

ANSWER: Any applicant who does not meet the criteria as listed above is not eligible for a permit to carry a pistol. The sheriff may also deny the application if there is a substantial likelihood that the applicant is a danger to himself/herself or others if issued a permit to carry.

QUESTION: Do I need to have my permit with me when carrying my pistol?

ANSWER: Yes, the permit holder must have the permit card and a valid driver's license, state identification card, or other government-issued photo identification in immediate possession at all times when carrying a pistol and must display the permit card and identification document when requested by a peace officer.

QUESTION: Where am I prohibited from carrying my pistol?

ANSWER: The provisions of federal and state law that describe these prohibitions are found at: Minnesota Statutes, section 243.55, Minnesota Statutes, section 609.66, Minnesota Statutes, section 624.714, Minnesota Statutes, section 641.165, 18 United States Code section 930

Permit Carriers:

Concealed Carry: All citizens shall be issued a carry permit.

Unconcealed Carry: Forbidden unless at established shooting events

Traveling with a Firearm: May transport loaded and concealed. Long arms can be transported loaded except during deer and turkey hunting seasons.

Notifying Law Enforcement of Carry Permit and Firearm: Only required if requested by an officer.

Self-Defense Model: Castle doctrine. Stand your ground.

Restaurants: May carry firearms in restaurants that do not have posted signs noting otherwise and as long as alcohol is not consumed.

Recognizes Carry Permits Issued by: All states

Law Uniformity: Local agencies cannot make additional restrictions upon state law.

All Citizens and Those Without Carry Permits:

Owning a Firearm: All citizens without license or permit

Owning a Semi-Auto: All citizens without license or permit

Owning a Machine Gun: All citizens without license or permit, must abide federal law

Carrying a Loaded Firearm in Public: Individuals must have a concealed handgun permit to carry a handgun. Long arms may be carried in most public areas and anywhere in a vehicle.

Traveling with a Firearm: Loaded handguns and long arms may be transported in anywhere in a vehicle, except during deer and turkey season when long arms must be transported unloaded.

State Parks: Only permit carriers may carry concealed weapons.

Gun Possession on College Campuses: Non-students with permits may bring guns on campus.

Additional Notes and Points of Interest: Businesses retain the right to forbid guns in their establishments, in which case individuals can legally store their firearms in a locked vehicle in the parking lot. Both permit carrier and non-permit carriers may store their loaded handgun anywhere in a vehicle.

FIREARM FRIENDLY:

Selective Excerpt From the State's Law:

<u>Frequently Asked Questions from the State's Department of Public Safety:</u>

QUESTION: How do I get a permit?

ANSWER: First time applications are now available at your nearest Highway Patrol Substation. There are substations located in Jackson, Greenwood, Batesville, New Albany, Starkville, Meridian, Hattiesburg, D'Iberville, and Brookhaven. Be sure to check "Firearm Permit Locations" for date & time of processing. MISSISSIPPI DOES NOT HAVE NON-RESIDENT PERMITS. Mississippi Law 45-9-101 (2) (a) states "The Department of Public Safety shall issue a license if the applicant: is a resident of the state and has been a resident for twelve (12) months or longer immediately preceding the filing of the application". NOTE: RENEWAL packets will continue to be mailed 90 days prior to expiration as stated in the statute. REMEMBER TO KEEP YOUR ADDRESS CURRENT. Please contact us regarding lost, misplaced or undelivered renewal packets.

QUESTION: How much does it cost to get an Individual Firearm Permit?

ANSWER: The fee for a first time Individual Firearm Permit is $132.00. The permit is valid for five (5) years. About 90 days prior to the permit's expiration date, a renewal package is sent to the permit holder. The renewal fee is $82.00. There is a $15 late fee for expired permits. A permit expired for six months or more is deemed permanently expired and the permit holder must reapply.

QUESTION: How long does it take to get permit after I apply?

ANSWER: Mississippi Law 45-9-101 (6) © "states the Department of Public Safety shall, within forty five (45) days after the date of receipt of the items listed in subsection (5) of this section:Issue the license: or Deny the application based solely on the ground that the applicant fails to meet the requirements.

QUESTION: What do I do if my address changes?

ANSWER: Within thirty (30) days after the changing of a permanent address, you must notify the Department of Public Safety in writing. The change of address should be mailed to the Firearm Permit Unit, P.O. Box 958, Jackson, MS 39205-0958. Be sure to include in your correspondence your name, permit number, old and new addresses, and a contact number in case of questions.

Contact for Additional Information:
Mississippi Highway Patrol/Gun Permits
P.O. Box 958 • Jackson, MS 39205-0958
601-987-1212

MISSOURI

Permit Carriers:

Concealed Carry: All citizens shall be issued a carry permit.

Unconcealed Carry: All citizens at least 21 years of age may carry a loaded handgun.

Traveling with a Firearm: May transport loaded handguns and long arms.

Notifying Law Enforcement of Carry Permit and Firearm: Only required if requested by an officer.

Self-Defense Model: Castle doctrine. Stand your ground only applies when in a vehicle.

Restaurants: May carry firearms in restaurants that do not have posted signs noting otherwise and as long as alcohol is not consumed.

Recognizes Carry Permits Issued by: All states

Law Uniformity: Local agencies may make additional restrictions upon state law, so being abreast with local law is important. Usually these additional laws restrict the unconcealed carry of firearms without a permit.

All Citizens and Those Without Carry Permits:

Owning a Firearm: All citizens without license or permit

Owning a Semi-Auto: All citizens without license or permit

Owning a Machine Gun: All citizens without license or permit, must abide federal law

Carrying a Loaded Firearm in Public: All citizens at least 21 years of age may carry a loaded, unconcealed handgun in public. Individuals should have his or her permit to carry a concealed weapon in public.

Traveling with a Firearm: All citizens at least 21 years of age or serving in the military may transport a loaded, concealed or unconcealed firearm anywhere in their vehicle. Those under 21 should transport handguns unloaded and cased. For individuals under 21, long arms can be carried loaded if they remain in plain view, unloaded if concealed.

State Parks: Only permit carriers may carry concealed weapons.

Gun Possession on College Campuses: Determined by college administration

Additional Notes and Points of Interest: Individuals should be at least 21 years of age before carrying or transporting firearms. When carrying an unconcealed firearm without a permit, ensure the local or city government hasn't established ordnances that forbid said action. Individuals with out-of-state permits may carry a concealed weapon in most instances. All military personnel 18 years or older may transport a loaded, concealed firearm in their vehicle.

FIREARM FRIENDLY: A+

Selective Excerpt From the State's Law:

Owning and Maintaining a Concealed Weapon, Information Courtesy of the State.

A Missouri resident must be at least 21 years old to apply. A person who is at least 18 years old and is a member of the United States Armed Forces, or is honorably discharged from the U.S. Armed Forces, is a citizen of the United States and has assumed residency, and is stationed in Missouri may apply for a Missouri concealed carry endorsement. The spouse of a member of the U.S. Armed Forces stationed in Missouri who is 21 years old may also apply for a Missouri concealed carry endorsement. If you wish to obtain a concealed weapon endorsement, you must first complete a firearms safety course at least eight hours in length.

> **In 2013, Missouri legislators almost passed a law that would have allowed residents to own fully automatic machine guns and arrest and detain federal agents who might try to take those weapons away.**

Once the firearms safety course is completed, the next step is to apply for the certificate of qualification at your local sheriff's office. You must present a copy of the firearms training course certificate, complete an application, and pay a non-refundable fee of $100. You may apply only in the county in which you reside. The application to the local sheriff (or police chief, if applicable, in first class counties) will contain a sworn statement. This statement verifies the applicant: meets the age requirement, is a citizen of the United States, has assumed residency in Missouri or is an armed forces member or spouse stationed in Missouri, has not been convicted or pled guilty or nolo contendre to any felony, has no weapons-related misdemeanor conviction, has not been convicted within the past five years of a violent misdemeanor, has not been convicted of two or more misdemeanors involving DWI or possession or abuse of a controlled substance within the past five years, is not a fugitive, and is not currently charged with a felony.

Contact for Additional Information:
Attorney General of Missouri
207 West High St., P.O. Box 899 • Jefferson City, MO 65102
573-751-3321

Permit Carriers:

Concealed Carry: Issued with discretion by local sheriff offices.

Unconcealed Carry: All citizens at least 21 years of age may carry a loaded handgun when outside a city, town, or work camp.

Traveling with a Firearm: Individuals may transport loaded handguns and long arms.

Notifying Law Enforcement of Carry Permit and Firearm: Only required if requested by an officer.

Self-Defense Model: Castle doctrine. Stand your ground.

Restaurants: Forbidden for all

Recognizes Carry Permits Issued by: All states but Alabama, Delaware, Hawaii, Maine, New Hampshire, and Road Island

Law Uniformity: Local laws are largely uniform with state ordinances.

All Citizens and Those Without Carry Permits:

Owning a Firearm: All citizens without license or permit

Owning a Semi-Auto: All citizens without license or permit

Owning a Machine Gun: All citizens without license or permit must abide federal law.

Carrying a Loaded Firearm in Public: All citizens at least 21 years of age may carry a loaded, unconcealed handgun when outside a city, town, or work camp. Individuals hiking and participating in similar outdoor activities may carry a concealed firearm without a permit.

Traveling with a Firearm: Loaded handguns may be transported and stored anywhere in a person's vehicle. Long arms should be kept in a case or gun rack.

State Parks: Only permit carriers may carry concealed weapons.

Gun Possession on College Campuses: Determined by college administration

Additional Notes and Points of Interest: Local sheriffs must approve individuals who are 18 years and older for their carry permit. In vehicles, loaded weapons can be stored in glove boxes or center consoles.

Contact for Additional Information:
Attorney General of Montana 207 West High
215 North Sanders/ P.O. Box 201401 • Helena, MT 59620
406-444-2026

Selective Excerpt From the State's Law:

Permitting Procedure for Obtaining a Concealed Weapons Permit

Download an application

Call for an appointment (required): 256-6941

A. You must be at least 18 years of age and have been a resident of the State of Montana for at least six months.

B. Any Criminal convictions per the Montana Codes may result in denial of the permit, or any omissions of arrests and/ or convictions may result in denial of the permit.

C. It is REQUIRED BY LAW that you complete a certified firearms safety course before the application is submitted. EXAMPLE: Hunter's Safety, DD-214, or any other NRA Certified Instructed course. Proof of completion of such course can be a photocopy of certificate, an affidavit from the entity or instructor that conducted the course or a copy of any other document that attests to completion of the course and can be certified through contact with the entity or instructor that conducted the course.

D. Applications for Concealed Weapons Permits will be taken by appointment only. You may schedule an appointment with the Detectives Division by calling 256-6941. Download an application to fill out here.

E. Bring the application, completed but unsigned, and your proof of firearms certification at the time of your scheduled appointment to the Sheriff's Office Detective Division, 2550 3rd Avenue N. (Round Building), Billings, MT, 2nd floor.

F. Application fee for a new Concealed Weapons Permit is $55.00, and the fee for a Renewal is $30.00. This includes the $5.00 Administrative Research fee. Please bring exact cash or a personal check. This fee is non-refundable. Fingerprinting and photographs will be taken at this time and no applications will be accepted without an appointment.

G. Please allow sixty (60) days for approval of your permit. A permit is valid for four (4) years. You will not be reminded of your permits expiration. Sixty (60) days should be allowed for processing of new applications.

H. Renewals are handled in the same manner as new applications, and fingerprints and photographs will be retaken. Please call at least thirty (30) days prior to your expiration date to make your appointment. An appointment is required, and you must fill out a new application form for renewals.

NEBRASKA

Permit Carriers:

Concealed Carry: All citizens over 21 years old shall be issued a carry permit. Law only covers carrying concealed handguns.

Unconcealed Carry: Permitted by any citizens but local agencies can regulate use.

Traveling with a Firearm: Loaded handguns may be transported in a vehicle for self-defense purposes. Handguns can be concealed on a person or in the glove box. Shotguns should be transported unloaded and stored in plain view. Loaded rifles may be transported if kept in plain view, in a case, or stored in a trunk or rear compartment of a vehicle.

Notifying Law Enforcement of Carry Permit and Firearm: Immediately upon making contact with an officer.

Self-Defense Model: No castle doctrine. Duty to retreat in public

Restaurants: May carry firearms in restaurants that do not have posted signs noting otherwise and as long as alcohol is not consumed.

Recognizes Carry Permits Issued by: All states but Alabama, Delaware, Georgia, Indiana, Maryland, Massachusetts, Mississippi, New York, New Hampshire, Pennsylvania, South Dakota, Washington, Wisconsin

Law Uniformity: Local agencies cannot make additional restrictions to most aspects of the state's gun laws, but some ban the open carry of handguns.

All Citizens and Those Without Carry Permits:

Owning a Firearm: All citizens without license or permit expect when purchasing a weapon

Owning a Semi-Auto: All citizens without license or permit

Owning a Machine Gun: All citizens without license or permit, must abide federal law

Carrying a Loaded Firearm in Public: Any adult may carry an unconcealed handgun in public without a permit, however some local laws ban the practice. Long arms and concealed handguns should not be brought into public.

Traveling with Firearms: Loaded rifles may be transported if they are kept in plain view, in a case, or stored in a trunk or rear compartment of a vehicle.

State Parks: Only permit carriers

Gun Possession on College Campuses: Determined by college administration

Additional Notes and Points of Interest: It's important to note that individuals must travel with loaded rifles in plain view and shotguns unloaded in plain view or in a gun case. The state's carry permit only applies to handguns.

Selective Excerpt From the State's Law:

Frequently Asked Questions Courtesy of the State's Police Department.

QUESTION: Where can I apply for a concealed handgun permit?

ANSWER: You must apply in person at one of the Nebraska State Patrol Troop Area offices or at the Criminal Identification Division of the State Patrol. The addresses are as follows: Criminal Identification Office - 3800 NW 12th Street, Suite A- Lincoln; Troop A Headquarters - 4411 S. 108th St. - Omaha; Troop B Headquarters - 1401 Eisenhower Avenue - Norfolk; Troop C Headquarters - 3431 Old Potash Highway - Grand Island; Troop D Headquarters - 300 W. South River Road - North Platte; Troop E Headquarters - 4500 Avenue I - Scottsbluff. Please check with the office you are planning to visit as days and hours of availability vary. Some offices do not always have staff available for fingerprinting and notarizing applications.

QUESTION: What will I need to take with me when I apply for a permit?

ANSWER: You will need the completed and notarized application form, proper identification, proof of training, valid proof of citizenship, proof of vision, and the permit fee. These documents are explained more in the following questions.

QUESTION: What documentation will I need for proof of citizenship?

ANSWER: Valid proof of citizenship can be an original or certified copy of a state issued birth certificate showing birth in the United States, a copy of naturalization papers, a Certificate of Citizenship issued by the United States Immigration authorities, or a current or expired United States passport.

QUESTION: What will I need to take with me when I apply for a permit?

ANSWER: You will need the completed and notarized application form, proper identification, proof of training, valid proof of citizenship, proof of vision, and the permit fee. These documents are explained more in the following questions.

Contact for Additional Information:
Nebraska State Police
P.O. Box 94907 • Lincoln, NE 68509
402-471-4545

NEBRASKA

Permit Carriers:

Concealed Carry: All citizens shall be issued a carry permit.

Unconcealed Carry: Unrestricted but local agencies try and regulate use

Traveling with a Firearm: Loaded handguns may be transported when kept in plain view or in a glove box or center console. Long arms should be transported unloaded.

Notifying Law Enforcement of Carry Permit and Firearm: Only required if requested by an officer.

Self-Defense Model: Castle doctrine. Stand your ground.

Restaurants: Permit carriers may carry firearms in restaurants that do not have posted signs noting otherwise and as long as alcohol is not consumed.

Recognizes Carry Permits Issued by: Alaska, Arizona, Arkansas, Kansas, Kentucky, Louisiana, Michigan, Missouri, Nebraska, New Mexico, North Carolina, Ohio, Rhode Island, South Carolina, Tennessee, West Virginia

Law Uniformity: Local agencies can make some additional restrictions to aspects of the state's gun law.

All Citizens and Those Without Carry Permits:

Owning a Firearm: All citizens without license or permit

Owning a Semi-Auto: All citizens without license or permit

Owning a Machine Gun: All citizens without license or permit, must abide federal law.

Carrying a Loaded Firearm in Public: Unconcealed, loaded handgun carry is permitted for any citizen but in towns that have specifically banned the action. Handguns must remain in a holster. Permit carriers should not carry an unconcealed weapon in Las Vegas.

Traveling with a Firearm: Long arms must remain unloaded, while handguns may be openly carried or stored in a glove box and not on one's person.

State Parks: Only permit carriers

Gun Possession on College Campuses: Only permit carriers

Additional Notes and Points of Interest: Though the state prohibits local agencies and governments from interfering with many of the state wide firearm laws, permit carriers should use caution before bring an unconcealed handgun in public in both Las Vegas and Reno.

FIREARM FRIENDLY:

Selective Excerpt From the State's Law:

Information Regarding Concealed Carry Courtesy
of the State's Police Department.

Permits:
Concealed Firearm Permits are valid for a period of five years and can be
renewed for additional five year periods. A permit holder must carry the
permit together with proper identification whenever he or she is in actual
possession of the concealed firearm(s). The permit and proper identification
must be presented to a peace officer upon request. Failure to produce the
permit and proper identification carry a civil penalty of $25.00. Carrying a
concealed firearm without a permit is punishable by a category C felony.

Qualifications:
Any person who meets the following criteria may apply to the Las Vegas
Metropolitan Police Department for a concealed firearm permit: A Nevada
resident, an out-of-state resident who received firearms training in the state,
21 years of age or older, not prohibited from possessing a firearm by State or
Federal law, successfully completes an approved firearms course in Clark County
(paid for by applicant), pays the appropriate fees, and a detailed instruction
sheet will accompany the application package with a list of approved firearms
instructors for courses and weapon qualification. All completed applications
must be submitted in person at the Fingerprint Bureau of the LVMPD.

General Denial Criteria.
Applications can be denied for reasons outlined in the Nevada Revised
Statutes. Such reasons include: An outstanding warrant of arrest (including
Traffic), a felony conviction, judicially declared incompetent or insane,
habitual abuser of drugs or alcohol, a conviction for a violent crime including
a misdemeanor, a conviction for domestic violence or stalking, currently
subject to a restraining order, injunction, or other order of protection
involving domestic violence, currently on parole or probation, a pending
entry of a felony conviction or recent suspension of a sentence for a felony,
pending criminal charges, and false statements on the application.

Contact for Additional Information:
Nevada Department of Public Safety
5 Wright Way • Carson City, NV 8971
775-684-4808

Permit Carriers:

Concealed Carry: All citizens shall be issued a carry permit.

Unconcealed Carry: Unrestricted, does not require carry permit

Traveling with a Firearm: Loaded, concealed handguns can be transported on a person. Long arms should be transported unloaded and stored in a gun rack, case, or in a trunk or rear storage compartment. Magazines are not required to be emptied, just separated from the weapon.

Notifying Law Enforcement of Carry Permit and Firearm: Only required if requested by an officer.

Self-Defense Model: Castle doctrine. Stand your ground.

Restaurants: Permit carriers can carry firearms in restaurants that do not have posted signs noting otherwise and as long as alcohol is not consumed.

Recognizes Carry Permits Issued by: Alabama, Alaska, Arizona, Arkansas, Colorado, Florida, Georgia, Idaho, Indiana, Iowa, Kentucky, Louisiana, Michigan, Missouri, Mississippi, North Carolina, North Dakota, Oklahoma, Pennsylvania, Tennessee, Utah, Wyoming

Law Uniformity: Local agencies cannot make additional restrictions to the state's gun law.

All Citizens and Those Without Carry Permits:

Owning a Firearm: All citizens without license or permit

Owning a Semi-Auto: All citizens without license or permit

Owning a Machine Gun: All citizens without license or permit, must abide federal law.

Carrying a Loaded Firearm in Public: Unconcealed, loaded handgun carry is permitted for any citizen. Handguns should be visible in holsters on the hip.

Traveling with a Firearm: Handguns should be transported unloaded and can be stored in plain view, the glove box, or center console. Rounds should be cleared from the magazine. Long arms should be transported unloaded and stored in a gun rack, case, or in a trunk or rear storage compartment.

State Parks: Only permit carriers

Gun Possession on College Campuses: Dependent on college administration

Additional Notes and Points of Interest: New Hampshire is fairly gun friendly and individuals traveling through the state should have little difficulty if firearms are transported unloaded, cased, and separate from ammunition. Loaded firearms can be carried at game refuges.

FIREARM FRIENDLY: A+

Selective Excerpt From the State's Law:

Frequently Asked Questions Courtesy of the State's Department of Safety.

QUESTION: The NH Non-Resident Pistol License does not contain the wording "carry concealed." Can I "carry concealed" with this license?

ANSWER: Yes, a license issued under RSA 159:6 is a full privilege concealed carry license.

> Despite being in the Northeast, New Hampshire is fiercely pro-gun. In 2013, certain pro-gun groups butted heads with Republican Governor Chris Christie concerning is somewhat indifference stance on a series of proposed gun laws.

QUESTION: I would like to bring my handgun into New Hampshire, yet I don't have a license to carry concealed. How may I carry?

ANSWER: You may carry unloaded in your vehicle. Be sure that the ammunition is separate from the gun. You may carry loaded on your person. The weapon needs to be fully exposed. For example, it may not be concealed by a shirt or a jacket, or located in a backpack.You may carry unloaded and concealed on your person, so long as you do not possess any ammunition on your person. Please refer to RSA 159 for additional information.

QUESTION: How do I submit an address change on a NH Non-Resident Pistol License?

ANSWER: Please forward a letter to NH State Police, Permits and Licensing Unit, 33 Hazen Drive, Concord NH 03305 notifying us of the change of address, including the old and new address. If you would like to receive a license that reflects the new address, enclose a fee of $3.00 made out to State of New Hampshire - Treasurer.

Contact for Additional Information:
New Hampshire State Police
P.O. Box 94907 • Lincoln, NE 68509
402-471-4545

Permit Carriers:

Concealed Carry: Yes, but issued with extreme discretion

Unconcealed Carry: Yes, but only with carry permit

Traveling with a Firearm: Loaded handguns may be transported on a person

Notifying Law Enforcement of Carry Permit and Firearm: Only required if requested by an officer.

Self-Defense Model: No castle doctrine. Duty to retreat in public.

Restaurants: Permit carriers can carry firearms in restaurants that do not have posted signs noting otherwise and as long as alcohol is not consumed.

Recognizes Carry Permits Issued by: No states

Law Uniformity: Laws are uniformly anti-gun across the state.

All Citizens and Those Without Carry Permits:

Owning a Firearm: Heavily restricted, must have carry permit to purchase a handgun

Owning a Semi-Auto: Heavily restricted, assault weapon models are banned from the state

Owning a Machine Gun: Forbidden

Carrying a Loaded Firearm in Public: Forbidden without carry permit

Traveling with Handguns: Transportation of firearms in New Jersey is largely forbidden. The only exceptions are those in route to hunting locations, shooting ranges, or established gun expositions. Under these circumstances, a gun should be disassembled as much as possible, cased, and stored in a trunk or rear compartment.

State Parks: Forbidden

Gun Possession on College Campuses: Forbidden

Additional Notes and Points of Interest: Individuals should use extreme caution when bringing a weapon through the state. The state also bans 15 shot magazines, military style semi-autos, and hollow-point style ammunition. For information regarding the state's law, contact the agency listed below before entering the state with a firearm.

Contact for Additional Information:
New Jersey State Police
P.O.Box 7068 • W. Trenton, NJ 08628
609-882-2000

FIREARM FRIENDLY: D

Selective Excerpt From the State's Law:

N.J.A.C. 13:54-1.4 Applications for a firearms purchaser identification card and for a permit to purchase a handgun.

(a) Every person applying for a firearms purchaser identification card or for a permit to purchase a handgun shall furnish such information and particulars as are set forth in the application form designated STS-33. Forms can be obtained from municipal police departments, State Police stations and licensed retail firearms dealers.

(b) The applicant shall waive any statutory or other right of confidentiality relating to institutional confinement.

(c) The applicant shall provide the names and addresses of two reputable citizens personally acquainted with him as references.

(d) The application shall be signed by the applicant and the completed application, together with two sets of the applicant's fingerprints and fees as established by N.J.A.C. 13:59 in accordance with N.J.S.A. 53:1-20.5 et seq., a consent for mental health records search form designated SP 66 and a nonrefundable application fee of $ 5.00 for a firearms identification card and $ 2.00 for a permit to purchase a handgun, shall be submitted to the chief of police of an organized full-time police department in the municipality in which the applicant resides. If the municipality does not have an organized full-time police department, application shall be made to the State Police station servicing the municipality in which the applicant resides, or to any State Police station in the case of a nonresident.

(e) The chief of police of an organized full-time police department of the municipality where the applicant resides, or the Superintendent, when the applicant is a non-resident of this State or when the municipality does not have a full time department, shall accept and investigate applications for firearms purchaser identification cards and permits to purchase handguns.

(f) The fingerprints of any applicant shall be compared with any fingerprints maintained by the State Bureau of Identification and the Federal Bureau of Identification for the purpose of ascertaining the existence of any criminal record. The fingerprints shall be obtained and submitted for such comparison by the chief of police or the State Police, as the case may be.

(g) An applicant for a handgun purchase permit who possesses a valid firearms purchaser identification card, or who has previously obtained a handgun purchase permit from the samelicensing authority for which he or she was previously fingerprinted, and who provides an additional valid identification document of his or her identity, need not be fingerprinted again. In such cases, the chief of police or Superintendent shall otherwise fully investigate the applicant in accordance with this subchapter. The chief of police or Superintendent shall require the applicant to complete the New Jersey State Police, State Bureau of Identification (SBI) "Request For Criminal History Record Information For Non Criminal Justice Purpose" form, and pay the appropriate fee established by N.J.A.C. 13:59. Applicants unable to provide an additional valid identification document shall submit to fingerprinting.

(h) Applicants for a permit to purchase a handgun may apply for more than one permit per application. The number of permits requested and each permit number shall be entered in the spaces provided on the application.

(i) The chief of police or the Superintendent, as the case may be, shall either approve or disapprove the applications. Permits and cards shall be issued by the chief of police or the Superintendent to persons who are found to be qualified and who are not subject to any of the disabilities set forth by this subchapter.

Permit Carriers:

Concealed Carry: All citizens shall be issued a carry permit

Unconcealed Carry: Unrestricted but local agencies can regulate use

Traveling with a Firearm: Loaded firearms may be transported in a vehicle for self-defense purposes.

Notifying Law Enforcement of Carry Permit and Firearm: Only required if requested by an officer.

Self-Defense Model: No castle doctrine. Stand your ground in public.

Restaurants: Firearms are permitted in restaurants that do not have posted signs noting otherwise, don't serve hard alcohol, and as long as alcohol is not consumed.

Recognizes Carry Permits Issued by: Arizona, Arkansas, Colorado, Delaware, Florida, Kansas, Louisiana, Michigan, Mississippi, Missouri, Nebraska, North Carolina, North Dakota, Ohio, Oklahoma, Tennessee, Texas, Virginia, West Virginia

Law Uniformity: Local agencies cannot make additional restrictions to most aspects of the state's gun law

All Citizens and Those Without Carry Permits:

Owning a Firearm: All citizens without license or permit

Owning a Semi-Auto: All citizens without license or permit

Owning a Machine Gun: All citizens without license or permit, must abide federal law

Carrying a Loaded Firearm in Public: All citizens over 21 years old may carry a loaded, holstered, unconcealed firearm in public. Firearms should not be brought into establishments that sell and serve alcohol.

Traveling with a Firearm: Loaded, both concealed and unconcealed, firearms may be transported anywhere in a vehicle.

State Parks: Firearms must be unloaded

Gun Possession on College Campuses: Dependent on administration, but forbidden for anyone over 19 years old regardless.

Additional Notes and Points of Interest: Only those 19 years or older can posses a handgun. A permit carrier should also avoid bringing a firearm into any establishment that sells and serves alcohol.

Contact for Additional Information:
New Mexico Dept. of Public Safety
6301 Indian School Rd. NE -#310 • Albuquerque, NM 87110
505-841-8053

Selective Excerpt From the State's Law:

Frequently Asked Questions Courtesy of the State's Department of Public Safety.

QUESTION: What do I need to include in my application for a Concealed Handgun Permit?

ANSWER: Complete application consists of eight items:

1) Complete two-page application
2) Photocopy of New Mexico Driver License of ID
3) $100.00 Application Fee (no cash)
4) Certified Original Birth Certificate**
5) Training Certificate
6) Two Fingerprint Cards, complete and signed
7) Health Information Release Form
8) Authorization for Release of Information

** Photocopies and/or Notarized copies will not suffice. If you would like your Birth Certificate returned include a self-addressed, stamped envelope in your packet.

QUESTION: I understand that the Department of Public Safety has thirty days to issue my license from the time I submit my application, is this true?

ANSWER: No. Pursuant to Subsection A of NMSA 29-19-6, the department has thirty days after receiving a completed application and completing a background investigation, to either issue a license or deny the applicant. It could take up to ninety (90) days or more to complete a background investigation.

QUESTION: How long is my license valid?

ANSWER: Concealed handgun licenses are valid for a period of four years from the date of issue, unless the license is suspended or revoked. There is a requalification requirement at two years.

QUESTION: Can an owner of private property prohibit me from carrying my concealed handgun on his premise?

ANSWER: Yes. Pursuant to Subsection C of NMSA 1978 Section 29-19-12, any person lawfully in possession of private property may prohibit the carrying of concealed handguns on such private property by posting notice in accordance with NMSA 1978 Section 30-14-6 or by verbally notifying persons entering upon the property.

QUESTION: How long does it take to issue a license?

ANSWER: On average, it takes approximately eight to twelve weeks to complete a background investigation before we can process the final license applications.

QUESTION: If I have my gun holstered in "plain view" on my belt will I be breaking the law?

ANSWER: New Mexico is an Open Carry State, meaning it is legal to carry a loaded weapon as long as it is not concealed. However, it is not legal to carry any firearm in any federal building or school. It is the responsibility of the person carrying the firearm to be informed as to when/where carrying is prohibited.

Permit Carriers:

New York City -

Concealed Carry: Yes, but issued with extreme discretionn

Unconcealed Carry: Forbidden

Traveling with a Firearm: Handguns may be carried with a permit. Long arms should always be unloaded and stored in a case.

Notifying Law Enforcement of Carry Permit and Firearm: Only required if requested by an officer

Self-Defense Model: No castle doctrine. Duty to retreat in public.

Restaurants: May carry firearms in restaurants that do not have posted signs noting otherwise and as long as alcohol is not consumed.

Recognizes Carry Permits Issued by: No states

Law Uniformity: Local laws exist, but are most common in New York City.

All Citizens and Those Without Carry Permits:

Owning a Firearm: Need license for handgun purchase. No permit needed for long arm possession.

Owning a Semi-Auto: Only assault rifle models produced before 1994 are forbidden, otherwise a license is not needed.

Owning a Machine Gun: Forbidden

Carrying a Loaded Firearm in Public: Forbidden without permit

Traveling with a Firearm: Largely forbidden. Individuals without a permit should carry any firearm unloaded, locked in a secure case, and stored in a trunk or rear storage compartment. Individuals should only bring firearms into the state when passing through and should not make extended stays in the state.

State Parks: Forbidden

Gun Possession on College Campuses: Forbidden

Additional Notes and Points of Interest: With rare exceptions, firearms aren't allowed in New York City. Persons traveling through the city may only have their unloaded and locked gun in the city for no more than 24 hours. Anyone without a license issued by the state should use extreme caution when traveling through New York, as their laws are unfriendly towards guns and gun owners. 10 round magazines are illegal as well as semi-automatic weapons produced before 1994. Individuals should check with the state before bringing a weapon into or through the state.

NEW YORK

Selective Excerpt From the State's Law:

License firearms Class A and B; conditions and restrictions

DEFENSE OF JUSTIFICATION: As a pistol licensee you are required to understand the laws relating to the use of deadly physical force. This chapter, titled Defense of Justification, is meant to inform you about "deadly physical force," specifically force caused by the use of a firearm.

USE OF PHYSICAL FORCE IN DEFENSE OF A PERSON

(NYS Penal Law Section 35.15)

1. A person may, subject to the provisions of subdivision two, use physical force upon another person when and to the extent he reasonably believes such to be necessary to defend himself or a third person from what he reasonably believes to be the use or imminent use of unlawful physical force by such other person, unless:

(a) The latter's conduct was provoked by the actor himself with intent to cause physical injury to another person; or

(b) The actor was the initial aggressor; except that in such case his use of physical force is nevertheless justifiable if he has withdrawn from the encounter and effectively communicated such withdrawal to such other person but the latter persists in continuing the incident by the use or threatened imminent use of unlawful physical force; or

(c) The physical force involved is the product of a combat by agreement not specifically authorized by law.

2. A person may not use deadly physical force upon another person under circumstances specified in subdivision one unless:

(a) He reasonably believes that such other person is using or is about to use deadly physical force. Even in such case however, the actor may not use deadly physical force if he knows that he can with complete safety as to himself and others avoid the necessity of so doing by retreating; except that he is under no duty to retreat if he is: (i) In his dwelling and not the initial aggressor; or (ii) A

Contact for Additional Information:
New York State Police
1220 Washington Ave., Bldg. 22 • Albany, NY 12226
518-783-3211

police officer or peace officer or a person assisting a police officer or a peace officer at the latter's direction, acting pursuant to Section 35.30 NYS Penal Law; or

New York City -

(b) He reasonably believes that such other person is committing or attempting to commit a kidnapping, forcible rape, forcible criminal act or robbery; or

(c) He reasonably believes that such other person is committing or attempting to commit a burglary, and the circumstances are such that the use of deadly physical force is authorized by subdivision three of Section 35.20 NYS Penal Law.

USE OF PHYSICAL FORCE IN DEFENSE OF PREMISES AND IN DEFENSE OF A PERSON IN THE COURSE OF A BURGLARY (Penal Law Section 35.20)

1. Any person may use physical force upon another person when he reasonably believes such to be necessary to prevent or terminate what he reasonably believes to be the commission or attempted commission by such other person of a crime involving damage to premises. He may use any degree of physical force, other than deadly physical force, which he reasonably believes to be necessary for such purpose, and he may use deadly physical force if he reasonably believes such to be necessary to prevent or terminate the commission or attempted commission of arson.

2. A person in possession or control of any premises, or a person licensed or privileged to be thereon or therein, may use physical force upon another person when he reasonably believes such to be necessary to prevent or terminate what he reasonably believes to be the commission or attempted commission by such other person of a criminal trespass upon such premises. He may use any degree of physical force, other than deadly physical force, which he reasonably believes to be necessary for such purpose, and he may use deadly physical force in order to prevent or terminate the commission or attempted commission of arson, as prescribed in subdivision one, or in the course of a burglary or attempted burglary, as prescribed in subdivision three.

3. A person in possession or control of, or licensed or privileged to be in, a dwelling or an occupied building, who reasonably believes that another person is committing or attempting to commit a burglary of such dwelling or building, may use deadly physical force upon such other person when he reasonably believes such to be necessary to prevent or terminate the commission or attempted commission of such burglary.

4. As used in this section, the following terms have the following meanings:

(a) The terms "premises," "building" and "dwelling" have the meanings prescribed in Section 140.00 NYS Penal Law.

(b) Persons "licensed or privileged" to be in buildings or upon other premises include, but are not limited to, police officers or peace officers acting in the performance of their duties.

USE OF PHYSICAL FORCE TO PREVENT OR TERMINATE LARCENY OR CRIMINAL MISCHIEF

(Penal Law Section 35.25)

A person may use physical force, other than deadly physical force, upon another person when and to the extent that he reasonably believes such to be necessary to prevent or terminate what he reasonably believes be the commission or attempted commission by such other person of larceny or of criminal mischief with respect to property other than premises.

USE OF PHYSICAL FORCE IN MAKING AN ARREST OR IN PREVENTING AN ESCAPE

(Penal Law Section 35.30)

3. A person who has been directed by a police officer or a peace officer to assist such police officer or peace officer to effect an arrest or to prevent an escape from custody may use physical force, other than deadly physical force, when and to the extent that he reasonably believes such to be necessary to carry out such police officer or peace officer's direction, unless he knows that the arrest or prospective arrest is not or was not authorized and he may use deadly physical force under such circumstances when:

(a) He reasonably believes such to be necessary to defend himself or a third person from what he reasonably believes to be the use or imminent use of deadly physical force; or

(b) He is directed or authorized by such police officer or peace officer to use deadly physical force unless he knows that the police officer or peace officer himself is not authorized to use deadly physical force under the circumstances.

4. A private person acting on his own account may use physical force, other than deadly physical force, upon another person when and to the extent that he reasonably believes such to be necessary to effect an arrest or to prevent the escape from custody of a person whom he reasonably believes to have committed an offense and who in fact has committed such offense; and he may use deadly physical force for such purpose when he reasonably believes such to be necessary to:

(a) Defend himself or a third person from what he reasonably believes to be the use or imminent use of deadly physical force; or

(b) Affect the arrest of a person who has committed murder, manslaughter in the first degree, robbery, forcible rape or forcible criminal sexual act and who is in immediate flight therefrom.

IT IS IMPORTANT TO NOTE THAT CHANGES IN THE LAW CONCERNING THE USE OF PHYSICAL FORCE AND DEADLY PHYSICAL FORCE MAY BE MADE FROM TIME TO TIME. YOU ARE RESPONSIBLE TO KNOW THE CURRENT LAWS.

Permit Carriers:

Concealed Carry: All citizens shall be issued a carry permit.

Unconcealed Carry: Unrestricted except at certain public functions

Traveling with a Firearm: Loaded, concealed handguns may be transported in a vehicle for self-defense purposes. Handguns can be concealed on a person or in the glove box. Long arms may be transported loaded and in plain view or unloaded and cased in a storage compartment. No permit is required to carry an unconcealed handgun.

Notifying Law Enforcement of Carry Permit and Firearm: Immediately upon contact with an officer.

Self-Defense Model: Castle doctrine. Stand your ground in public.

Restaurants: Forbidden for all

Recognizes Carry Permits Issued by: All states

Law Uniformity: Local agencies cannot make additional restrictions to the state's gun law.

All Citizens and Those Without Carry Permits:

Owning a Firearm: All citizens without license or permit, expect for the purchase of handguns

Owning a Semi-Auto: All citizens without license or permit

Owning a Machine Gun: Requires permit from sheriff, must abide federal law

Carrying a Loaded Firearm in Public: Unconcealed, loaded handguns carry is unrestricted except at certain public functions.

Traveling with a Firearm: Loaded handguns may be transported in a vehicle for self-defense purposes if they remain in plain view or on a visible side holster. It is also acceptable if loaded handguns are locked in a glove box or console, but this is not advised. Long arms should be unloaded and cased while in transport.

State Parks: Only permit carriers

Gun Possession on College Campuses: Forbidden

Additional Notes and Points of Interest: The state's carry permit only covers concealed handguns. Individuals may openly carry firearms while hunting or target shooting without a carry permit.

FIREARM FRIENDLY: A+

Selective Excerpt From the State's Law:

B. North Carolina Requirements.

North Carolina's pistol permitting and concealed carry permit laws qualify as an alternative to the requirements of the Brady Law. Therefore, when a person desires to purchase a handgun from a federally-licensed dealer, the person needs to comply solely with North Carolina's pistol permit laws, and present a valid permit to purchase a handgun or valid North Carolina-issued concealed carry permit. (Please note: Even if a NICS inquiry by a federally-licensed dealer was done in this circumstance, it does not do away with the necessity for a pistol purchase permit.) As always, any other transfer between private individuals is also governed by North Carolina's pistol permit laws.

Under North Carolina law, it is unlawful for any person, firm, or corporation to sell, give away, transfer, purchase, or receive, at any place in the state, any pistol, unless the purchaser or receiver has first obtained a license or permit to receive such a pistol by the sheriff of the county where the purchaser or receiver resides, or the purchaser or receiver possesses a valid North

Carolina-issued concealed carry permit. This requirement to obtain a permit prior to the transfer of a pistol applies not only to a commercial transaction typically at a sporting goods store but also between private individuals or companies throughout North Carolina. N.C. Gen. Stat. § 14-402(a).

In addition, this State law has been interpreted to require that a pistol permit be obtained by the receiver of a handgun when a person inherits a pistol as a result of the death of another person. The permit should be given to and retained by the seller or donor of the handgun. In such a case, the permit should be given to the executor or receiver of the estate of the deceased person. If the purchaser or receiver uses a North Carolina- issued concealed carry permit for the transfer, the seller should reference such permit on a bill of sale.

Further, it is unlawful for any person to receive from any postmaster, postal clerk, employee in the parcel post department, rural mail carrier, express agent or employee, or railroad agent or employee, within the State of North Carolina, any pistol without having in his or her possession, such a pistol purchase permit or North Carolina concealed carry permit.

Contact for Additional Information:
Attorney General of North Carolina
9001 Mail Service Center • Raleigh, NC 27699
919-716-6400

Permit Carriers:

Concealed Carry: All citizens shall be issued a carry permit.

Unconcealed Carry: Permitted with a carry permit

Traveling with a Firearm: Loaded handguns may be transported on a person. Long arms should be unloaded and in open view while in transport.

Notifying Law Enforcement of Carry Permit and Firearm: Only required if requested by an officer.

Self-Defense Model: Castle doctrine. Stand your ground.

Restaurants: Forbidden

Recognizes Carry Permits Issued by: Alabama, Alaska, Arizona, Arkansas, Colorado, Delaware, Florida, Georgia, Idaho, Indiana, Iowa, Kansas, Kentucky, Louisiana, Maine, Michigan, Missouri, Montana, Nebraska, New Hampshire, New Mexico, North Carolina, Ohio, Oklahoma, Pennsylvania, South Carolina, South Dakota, Tennessee, Texas, Utah, Virginia, Washington, West Virginia, Wisconsin, Wyoming

Law Uniformity: Local agencies cannot make additional restrictions to most aspects of the state's gun law.

All Citizens and Those Without Carry Permits:

Owning a Firearm: All citizens without license or permit

Owning a Semi-Auto: All citizens without license or permit

Owning a Machine Gun: All citizens without license or permit, must abide federal law

Carrying a Loaded Firearm in Public: Unloaded handguns may be carried during daylight hours as long as they remain unloaded and rounds clear from the magazine. All persons may carry a loaded handgun while hunting or target shooting.

Traveling with Firearms: Firearms may be unloaded and in open view while in transport. They may also be stored unloaded and cased in a trunk or rear compartment. Unloaded handguns may be stored in unconcealed side holsters while being transported, but not in a glove box or center console.

State Parks: Only permit carriers

Gun Possession on College Campuses: Forbidden

Additional Notes and Points of Interest: A resident only needs to be 18 years old to apply for his or her carry permit. Firearms are not permitted at any public gathering or meeting, such as sporting events, school activities, or concerts. The state allows firearms to be kept in vehicles at locations where firearms are not allowed, such as the mentioned events and restaurants.

Contact for Additional Information:
Attorney General of North Dakota
Dept. 125/ 600 East Blvd. Ave. • Bismark, ND 58505
701-328-2210

FIREARM FRIENDLY: A

Selective Excerpt From the State's Law:

Eligibility for a Concealed Weapon License.

Concealed weapon licenses may be issued only to individuals who legally can possess a firearm/dangerous weapon. Individuals may be prohibited by state or federal law from owning, possessing, or having a firearm under their control. For more information, contact an attorney in private practice. To be eligible to apply for a North Dakota Concealed Weapon License, you:

1. Must legally be able to possess a firearm/dangerous weapon; and

2. At least age 21 (for a Class 1 License), or at least age 18 (for a Class 2 License); and

3. Either a US Citizen OR a legal alien residing in the United States; and

4. Your state of residence is determined by your driver's license. If you are not a ND resident, you must have a valid concealed weapon license from your home state, which state must have reciprocity with ND; and

5. For a Class 1 license, you cannot have been convicted of any offense involving the use of alcohol (e.g.: MIP, MIC, open container, DUI) within 10 years prior to the date of application or renewal application. If you have an alcohol offense within the past 10 years, you may apply only for a Class 2 license.

ALL APPLICANTS:

(1) Two passport photographs–write your name on the back of each photograph; The BCI will not accept alternate or substitute photographs. For the photograph, applicants may not wear glasses (including prescription eye glasses), hats, scarves, head coverings, uniforms, or any items that obscure the facial features. For complete instructions, refer to the Administrative Rules on the Concealed Weapons License page (under "Read the Law"). Photographs that do not conform to the BCI requirements will be rejected and the application will be returned to applicant.

(2) A photocopy of your current state driver's license or state issued non-driving identification card;

(3) The nonrefundable application processing fee.

AND, if applicable: NEW Applicants only-Fingerprints: In addition, you must submit a fingerprint card. Contact your local law enforcement agency or test administrator. Fingerprints are not required for renewal. There may be a separate charge for fingerprinting. NON-RESIDENT Applicants: State of residency is determined by your state-issued license/identification card. If you are a resident of a state that has reciprocity with North Dakota, you must possess a concealed carry/concealed weapon license from your home state and submit a copy of the valid license with your application for a ND license. If your home state does not have reciprocity with ND, you are not eligible for a ND concealed weapon license. For a list of reciprocal states, see: http://www.ag.nd.gov/BCI/CW/reciprocity.htm.

OHIO

Permit Carriers:

Concealed Carry: All citizens shall be issued a carry permit. Only handguns can be carried concealed.

Unconcealed Carry: Unrestricted for any citizen, both those with andwithout a carry permit

Traveling with a Firearm: All firearms should be transported unloaded and stored in a case or stored in plain view. The state doesn't allow permit carriers to travel with loaded firearms.

Notifying Law Enforcement of Carry Permit and Firearm: Immediately upon making contact with an officer.

Self-Defense Model: Castle doctrine. Stand your ground only in vehicles.

Restaurants: Permit carriers can carry firearms in restaurants that do not have posted signs noting otherwise and as long as alcohol is not consumed.

Recognizes Carry Permits Issued by: Alaska, Arizona (residents only), Arkansas, Delaware, Florida, Idaho, Kansas, Kentucky, Louisiana, Michigan, Missouri, Nebraska, New Mexico, North Carolina, North Dakota, Oklahoma, South Carolina, Tennessee, Utah, Virginia, Washington, West Virginia, Wyoming

Law Uniformity: Local agencies cannot make additional restrictions to most aspects of the state's gun law. Any additional law made by a local agency cannot be legally enforced.

All Citizens and Those Without Carry Permits:

Owning a Firearm: All citizens without license or permit

Owning a Semi-Auto: All citizens without license or permit, but magazines that hold 31 or more rounds are forbidden.

Owning a Machine Gun: All citizens without a license or permit, but must be securely stored and must abide federal law.

Carrying a Loaded Firearm in Public: Individuals with and without a carry permit can carry an unconcealed handgun in public, but the practice is relatively uncommon in the state.

Traveling with Firearms: All firearms should be transported unloaded and stored in a case or stored in plain view. The state doesn't allow permit carriers to travel with loaded firearms.

State Parks: Only permit carriers

Gun Possession on College Campuses: Forbidden under most circumstances

Additional Notes and Points of Interest: The state defines a gun to be loaded if there are rounds in a detached magazine. Individuals should travel with ammunition stored in commercial grade ammo boxes in a different location in a vehicle from firearms. It should again be noted that individuals with carry permits may not travel with a loaded firearm under any circumstance. Guns should be transported unloaded and stored in a case.

FIREARM FRIENDLY: A

Selective Excerpt From the State's Law:

<u>Sheriff's Criteria for Issuing the License.</u>

1. Residency- You must be a legal resident of the United States and an Ohio resident for 45 days before you apply for your license. You must be a resident of the county (or adjoining county) where you apply for at least 30 days. You also must be at least 21 years of age and not a fugitive from justice.

2. Residency for Members of the Armed Forces- You are considered an Ohio resident for purposes of obtaining and renewing a license to carry a concealed handgun if you are absent from the country, Ohio, or an Ohio county while complying with military or naval orders as an active or reserve member of the armed forces of the United States. Prior to leaving this state in compliance with those orders, you must be legally living in the United States and be a resident of this state. Solely by reason of that absence, you are not considered to have lost your status as living in the United States or your residence in this state or in the county in which you were a resident prior to leaving this state in compliance with those orders. This is without regard to whether or not you intend to return to this state or to your county. You shall not be considered to have acquired residence in any other state and shall not be considered to have become a resident of any other state. If you are present in this state in compliance with military or naval orders as an active or reserve member of the armed forces of the United States for at least 45 days, you are considered to have been a resident of this state for at least 45 days.

3. Criminal Record- Prior to obtaining your license, you must provide the sheriff with complete information about your background. There are many criminal offenses that bar you from obtaining a license. There are many laws and conditions that prohibit you from owning a handgun. If you have questions about spastics??, you should consult an attorney.

4. Mental Competency
The law states that you must not have been adjudicated as a mental defective, committed to any mental institution, under a current adjudication of incompetence, found by a court to be mentally ill subject to hospitalization by court order, or an involuntary patient other than one who is a patient only for purposes of observation.

5. Protection Orders
You must not be subject to a civil protection order or a temporary protection order of an Ohio court or a similar protection order issued by another state. For additional information on civil and temporary protection orders, consult an attorney. As long as you meet the law's requirements, the sheriff must issue a concealed handgun license within 45 days of receiving your properly completed application. The license lasts for five years.

Contact for Additional Information:
Attorney General of Ohio
30 East Broad Street- 17th Floor • Columbus, OH 43215
800-282-0515

Permit Carriers:

Concealed Carry: All citizens shall be issued a carry permit, but limited to .45 calibers or weaker calibers.

Unconcealed Carry: Acceptable with carry permit, but limited to .45 or weaker calibers.

Traveling with a Firearm: Loaded handguns may be transported in a vehicle for self-defense purposes. Handguns can be concealed on a person or in the glove box. Long arms should be unloaded while in transport.

Notifying Law Enforcement of Carry Permit and Firearm: Immediately upon making contact with an officer.

Self-Defense Model: Castle doctrine. Stand your ground.

Restaurants: Permit carriers can carry firearms in restaurants that do not have posted signs noting otherwise and as long as alcohol is not consumed.

Recognizes Carry Permits Issued by: All states

Law Uniformity: Local agencies cannot make additional restrictions to the state's gun law

All Citizens and Those Without Carry Permits:

Owning a Firearm: All citizens without license or permit

Owning a Semi-Auto: All citizens without license or permit

Owning a Machine Gun: All citizens without a license or permit must abide federal law.

Carrying a Loaded Firearm in Public: Forbidden without carry permit

Traveling with Firearms: All handguns must be unloaded and in open view, in a gun case, or in a trunk or rear compartment, but not a glove box or center console. Unloaded handguns transported in plain view should be at least partially visible from outside the vehicle. Long arms should be transported in plain view or kept behind the passenger seats. Those from states that do not require carry permits to carry a concealed firearm may legally carry a concealed firearm in Oklahoma.

State Parks: Only permit carriers

Gun Possession on College Campuses: Permitted for any gun owner

Additional Notes and Points of Interest: The state's laws allow individuals with a firearm to legally store their firearm in their vehicle while at a prohibited location, like a public sporting event.

FIREARM FRIENDLY: A

Selective Excerpt From the State's Law:

TITLE 21 § 1290.9 ELIGIBILITY (for concealed carry permit).

The following requirements shall apply to any person making application to the Oklahoma State Bureau of Investigation for a handgun license pursuant to the provisions of the Oklahoma Self-Defense Act. The person must:

1. Be a citizen of the United States;

2. Establish a residency in the State of Oklahoma. For purposes of the Oklahoma Self-Defense Act, the term residency shall apply to any person who either possesses a valid Oklahoma driver license or state photo identification card, and physically maintains a residence in this state or has permanent military orders within this state and possesses a valid driver license from another state where such person claims residency;

> **In 2012, gun advocates in the state celebrated when legislators passed bills allowing those with their concealed carry permit to also carry unconcealed weapons in public.**

3. Be at least twenty-one (21) years of age;

4. Complete a firearms safety and training course and demonstrate competence and qualifications with the type of pistol to be carried by the person as provided in Section 1290.14 of this title, and submit proof of training and qualification or an exemption for training and qualification as authorized by Section 1290.14 of this title;

5. Submit the required fee and complete the application process as provided in Section 1290.12 of this title; and

6. Comply in good faith with the provisions of the Oklahoma Self-Defense Act.

Contact for Additional Information:
Oklahoma Bureau of Investigation
6600 N. Harvey • Oklahoma City, Oklahoma 73116
405-848-6724

Permit Carriers:

Concealed Carry: All citizens shall be issued a carry permit.

Unconcealed Carry: Unrestricted but local agencies may regulate use

Traveling with a Firearm: Loaded handguns may be transported in a vehicle if the weapon is visible on a belt holster. Loaded handguns may not be transported concealed or readily available off a person. Otherwise, handguns may be stored in a vehicle's trunk while also in a case. If the vehicle doesn't have a trunk, handguns may be locked in a glove box or center console. The key shouldn't be left in the lock. Loaded long arms may be stored in gun racks, cases, or in a trunk of a vehicle.

Notifying Law Enforcement of Carry Permit and Firearm: Only required if requested by an officer.

Self-Defense Model: No castle doctrine. Stand your ground in public.

Restaurants: Permit carriers can carry firearms in restaurants that do not have posted signs noting otherwise and as long as alcohol is not consumed.

Recognizes Carry Permits Issued by: No states

Law Uniformity: Local agencies cannot make additional restrictions to most aspects of the state's gun law.

All Citizens and Those Without Carry Permits:

Owning a Firearm: All citizens without license or permit

Owning a Semi-Auto: All citizens without license or permit

Owning a Machine Gun: All citizens without license or permit, must abide federal law

Carrying a Loaded Firearm in Public: Those with and without a carry permit may carry an unconcealed handgun in public, but the practice is forbidden in most metropolitan localities.

Traveling with Firearms: Loaded firearms should be transported in plain view or in a trunk or rear storage compartment of a vehicle.

State Parks: Only permit carriers

Gun Possession on College Campuses: Only permit carriers

Additional Notes and Points of Interest: Cities may ban the open carry of firearms, such as Portland has done. Both permit carriers and non-permit carriers may carry a concealed handgun on a motorcycle, ATV, or similar personal motorized vehicle, but the gun's trigger should be locked or the gun kept in a locked case. The state allows anyone staying in a parked RV being used as a primary residence to keep a loaded handgun in the vehicle. This does not apply when the RV is in motion and the laws revert back to normal.

FIREARM FRIENDLY: A

Selective Excerpt From the State's Law:

Concealed Handgun License.

To obtain a concealed handgun license, you must:

1. Be able to demonstrate competence with a handgun by showing a certificate or written statement that you have been trained by: A handgun safety course utilizing either police instructors or those certified by the NRA, including courses provided for security guards, reserve police officers, law enforcement officers, military service and organized shooting competition; or

A hunter education safety course approved by the State Department of Fish and Wildlife; or

You hold a previous Oregon license to carry a concealed handgun.

2. Be a citizen of the United States of America. If you were not born a citizen of the United States, you must provide proof of citizenship, i.e., a U.S. Passport, Certification of Naturalization, or, if you were born on a military base, a Birth Certificate. If you are a legal resident alien, you must document continuous residency in Marion County for at least six months and declare in writing to the Immigration and Naturalization Service your intention to become a citizen and provide such proof of the written declaration to the Sheriff at the time of application for a concealed handgun license;

3. Have your principal residence in Marion County;

4. Have your current address on your driver's license;

5. Be at least 21 years of age;

6. Have been discharged from the jurisdiction of a juvenile court for more than four years if you were under their jurisdiction for committing an act which, if committed by an adult, would have constituted a felony or a misdemeanor.

Contact for Additional Information:
Attorney General or Oregon
1162 Court Street NE • Salem, OR 97301
503-378-4400

Permit Carriers:

Concealed Carry: All citizens shall be issued a carry permit.

Unconcealed Carry: Unrestricted for anyone with or without a carry permit

Traveling with a Firearm: Loaded, concealed handguns may be transported on a person. Long arms should be kept unloaded while in transport.

Notifying Law Enforcement of Carry Permit and Firearm: Only required if requested by an officer.

Self-Defense Model: Castle doctrine. Stand your ground.

Restaurants: Permit carriers can carry firearms in restaurants that do not have posted signs noting otherwise and as long as alcohol is not consumed.

Recognizes Carry Permits Issued by: Alaska, Arizona, Colorado, Florida, Georgia, Idaho, Indiana, Iowa, Kentucky, Louisiana, Maine, Michigan, Missouri, Mississippi, Montana, New Hampshire, North Carolina, North Dakota, Oklahoma, South Dakota, Tennessee, Texas, Utah, Virginia, West Virginia, Wisconsin, Wyoming

Law Uniformity: Local agencies cannot make additional restrictions to most aspects of the state's gun law

All Citizens and Those Without Carry Permits:

Owning a Firearm: All citizens without license or permit

Owning a Semi-Auto: All citizens without license or permit

Owning a Machine Gun: All citizens without license or permit, must abide federal law

Carrying a Loaded Firearm in Public: Unrestricted for anyone with or without a carry permit to carry an unconcealed handgun in public but the handgun should remain visible on a side holster.

Traveling with a Firearm: Handguns should be unloaded, cased, and kept in a rear compartment or trunk out of reach from passengers. Ammunition should also be clearly separated from any firearm. Long arms should be transported unloaded.

State Parks: Only permit carriers

Gun Possession on College Campuses: Dependent on college administration

Additional Notes and Points of Interest: Unconcealed carry for both those with and without a carry permit is forbidden in Philadelphia. Unconcealed long arms should not be brought into public.

FIREARM FRIENDLY: A+

Selective Excerpt From the State's Law:

Carrying Firearms in Pennsylvania, Courtesy of Pennsylvania State Police.

QUESTION: Who can apply for a Pennsylvania License to Carry?

ANSWER: An individual who is 21 years of age or older may apply for a license to carry firearms by submitting a completed Application for a Pennsylvania License to Carry Firearms to the sheriff of the county in which they reside or if a resident of a city of the first class, with the chief of police of that city along with the required fee.

Individuals who are 21 years of age or older and are NOT Pennsylvania residents may apply for a license by submitting a completed Application for a Pennsylvania License to Carry Firearms to any Pennsylvania County Sheriff's office along with the required fee. A Pennsylvania license cannot be issued to a resident of another state who does not possess a current license or permit or similar document to carry a firearm issued by their home state if a license is provided for by the laws of that state, as published annually in the Federal Register by the Bureau of Alcohol, Tobacco and Firearms of the Department of the Treasury.

The sheriff has 45 days to conduct an investigation to determine an individual's eligibility to be issued a license. Included in the investigation is a background check conducted on the individual through the Pennsylvania Instant Check System (PICS) to determine if the records indicate the individual is prohibited by law. In accordance with 18 PA C.S. §6109, a sheriff may deny an individual the right to a License to Carry Firearms if there is reason to believe that the character and reputation of the individual are such that they would be likely to act in a manner dangerous to public safety.

If the PICS check is approved and the subject is of good character, the sheriff may issue a License to Carry Firearms. The issuance of a License to Carry Firearms allows individuals to carry a firearm concealed on or about their person, or in a vehicle throughout this Commonwealth. The license is valid for a period of five (5) years unless sooner revoked.

NOTE: A license to carry firearms is NOT a license to purchase. Individuals who purchase a firearm from a licensed dealer are required to have a background check conducted regardless of whether they have a license to carry firearms or not.

Contact for Additional Information:
Attorney General of Pennsylvania
16th Floor/ Strawberry Square • Harrisburg, PA 17120
717-787-3391

Permit Carriers:

Concealed Carry: Issued with discretion

Unconcealed Carry: Mostly forbidden, requires a permit issued by the state's attorney general

Traveling with a Firearm: Firearms should be unloaded and cased or kept in a gun rack. Non-residents passing through the state with a handgun should also not stop their journey in the state for any extended amount of time apart from travel requirements.

Notifying Law Enforcement of Carry Permit and Firearm: Only required if requested by an officer.

Self-Defense Model: No castle doctrine. Duty to retreat in public.

Restaurants: May carry firearms in restaurants that do not have posted signs noting otherwise and as long as alcohol is not consumed.

Recognizes Carry Permits Issued by: No states

Law Uniformity: Local agencies cannot make additional restrictions to most aspects of the state's gun law.

All Citizens and Those Without Carry Permits:

Owning a Firearm: All citizens without license or permit

Owning a Semi-Auto: All citizens without license or permit

Owning a Machine Gun: Forbidden

Carrying a Loaded Firearm in Public: Forbidden without permit

Traveling with Firearms: Long arms should be unloaded and cased or kept in a gun rack. Handguns should be transported unloaded and cased with ammunition separately stored in the trunk or an outside storage compartment beyond the reach of passengers. Individuals transporting a firearm should also do so only between a shooting range, gun shop, or related gun event. Non-residents passing through the state with a handgun should not stop their journey in the state for any extended amount of time apart from travel requirements and should keep their firearm unloaded and cased with ammunition stored in the trunk or separate compartment away from passengers.

State Parks: Forbidden. Firearms may be kept unloaded and cased in a vehicle.

Gun Possession on College Campuses: Dependent on college administration

Additional Notes and Points of Interest: Proceed with caution when traveling through the state. It's recommended for individuals to disassemble and secure their firearm as much as possible as well as separate ammunition.

FIREARM FRIENDLY:

Selective Excerpt From the State's Law:

PISTOL PERMIT POLICY.

Pursuant to Rhode Island General Laws Section 11-47-11, the Burrillville Police Department has the authority to issue a license or permit to carry a concealed pistol or revolver to any person 21 years of age or over upon a proper showing of need, or has good reason to fear an injury to his or her person or property, or has any other proper reason for carrying a pistol or revolver, and that he or she is a suitable person to be so licensed. The Burrillville Police Department will exercise its discretion consistent with Section 11-47.11.

Pursuant to Rhode Island General Laws Section 11-47-15, the applicant must also qualify to obtain a permit. The right to carry a loaded, concealed firearm in public is different from the right to purchase or possess a handgun in one's own home or business. The Burrillville Police Department does not discriminate in the issuance of a pistol permit on grounds of race, sex, national origin, or any other reason prohibited by law.

PROCEDURE.

An applicant for a pistol permit must submit a written application with a recent photograph, two types of positive identification, and a full set of fingerprints on the FBI fingerprint applicant card to the Burrillville Police Department, 1477 Victory Highway, Oakland, RI 02858. The Burrillville Police Department then checks the applicant's background with state, local, and Federal law enforcement databases. The Burrillville Police Department may also check court records and other sources for pending criminal cases, restraining orders and/or discrepancies in the applicant's background, including prior history of mental illness. The Burrillville Police Department will not issue a pistol permit to any applicant who is prohibited from possessing or carrying a firearm under any state or Federal law (e.g. 18 U.S.C. Section 922(g)) or pursuant to any court order. If this initial check does not disqualify the applicant from obtaining a pistol permit, the Burrillville Police Department may conduct a personal interview to clarify information provided on the application.

Contact for Additional Information:
Attorney General of Rhode Island
150 S. Main Street • Providence, RI 02903
401-274-4400

Permit Carriers:

Concealed Carry: All citizens shall be issued a carry permit

Unconcealed Carry: Largely forbidden

Traveling with a Firearm: Loaded handguns can be transported on individuals with a carry permit. All persons with or without a permit may transport loaded long arms as well as loaded handguns as long as they remain in a glove box, center console, or trunk and not concealed on a person.

Notifying Law Enforcement of Carry Permit and Firearm: Immediately upon making contact with an officer.

Self-Defense Model: Castle doctrine. Stand your ground in public.

Restaurants: Forbidden

Recognizes Carry Permits Issued by: Alaska, Arizona, Arkansas, Florida, Kansas, Kentucky, Louisiana, Michigan, Missouri, North Carolina, Ohio, Oklahoma, Texas, Tennessee, Virginia, West Virginia, Wyoming

Law Uniformity: Local agencies cannot make additional restrictions to most aspects of the state's gun law.

All Citizens and Those Without Carry Permits:

Owning a Firearm: All citizens without license or permit

Owning a Semi-Auto: All citizens without license or permit

Owning a Machine Gun: All citizens without license or permit, must abide federal law

Carrying a Loaded Firearm in Public: Forbidden without permit except a loaded handgun when hunting and fishing with a license. A loaded handgun may also be carried in a motel room as long as the bill and tax in the room has been paid.

Traveling with Firearms: All persons with or without a permit may transport loaded long arms as well as loaded handguns as long as they remain in a glove box, center console, or trunk and not concealed on a person.

State Parks: Only permit carriers

Gun Possession on College Campuses: Forbidden

Additional Notes and Points of Interest: The only major exemption to the state's relaxed firearm transport laws is that loaded firearms are forbidden to be transported through wildlife areas during hunting season.

Contact for Additional Information:
South Carolina Law Enforcement Division
P.O. Box 21398 • Columbia, SC 29221
803-896-7015

Selective Excerpt From the State's Law:

<u>CONCEALED WEAPON PERMITS.</u>

SECTION 23-31-215. Issuance of permits.

(A) Notwithstanding any other provision of law, except subject to subsection (B) of this section, SLED must issue a permit, which is no larger than three and one half inches by three inches in size, to carry a concealable weapon to a resident or qualified nonresident who is at least twenty one years of age and who is not prohibited by state law from possessing the weapon upon submission of:

(1) a completed application signed by the person;

(2) one current full face color photograph of the person, not smaller than one inch by one inch nor larger than three inches by five inches;

(3) proof of residence or if the person is a qualified nonresident, proof of ownership of real property in this State;

(4) proof of actual or corrected vision rated at 20/40 within six months of the date of application or, in the case of a person licensed to operate a motor vehicle in this State, presentation of a valid driver's license;

(5) proof of training;

(6) payment of a fifty dollar application fee. This fee must be waived for disabled veterans and retired law enforcement officers; and

(7) a complete set of fingerprints unless, because of a medical condition verified in writing by a licensed medical doctor, a complete set of fingerprints is impossible to submit. In lieu of the submission of fingerprints, the applicant must submit the written statement from a licensed medical doctor specifying the reason or reasons why the applicant's fingerprints may not be taken. If all other qualifications are met, the Chief of SLED may waive the fingerprint requirements of this item. The statement of medical limitation must be attached to the copy of the application retained by SLED. A law enforcement agency may charge a fee not to exceed five dollars for fingerprinting an applicant.

(B) Upon submission of the items required by subsection (A) of this section, SLED must conduct or facilitate a local, state, and federal fingerprint review of the applicant. SLED must also conduct a background check of the applicant through notification to and input from the sheriff of the county where the applicant resides or if the applicant is a qualified nonresident, where the applicant owns real property in this State. The sheriff within ten working days after notification by SLED, must submit a recommendation on an application. Before making a determination whether or not to issue a permit under this article, SLED must consider the recommendation provided pursuant to this subsection. The failure of the sheriff to submit a recommendation within the ten day period constitutes a favorable recommendation for the issuance of the permit to the applicant. If the fingerprint review and background check are favorable, SLED must issue the permit.

SOUTH DAKOTA

Permit Carriers:

Concealed Carry: All citizens shall be issued a carry permit.

Unconcealed Carry: Unrestricted in most locations

Traveling with a Firearm: Loaded, concealed handguns may be transported in a vehicle. Long arm transportation is largely unrestricted but long arm firearms should be cased when passing through a game or nature reserves.

Notifying Law Enforcement of Carry Permit and Firearm: Only required if requested by an officer.

Self-Defense Model: Castle doctrine. Stand your ground in public.

Restaurants: Permit carriers can carry firearms in restaurants that do not have posted signs noting otherwise and as long as alcohol is not consumed.

Recognizes Carry Permits Issued by: All states

Law Uniformity: Local agencies cannot make additional restrictions to the state's gun law

All Citizens and Those Without Carry Permits:

Owning a Firearm: All citizens without license or permit

Owning a Semi-Auto: All citizens without license or permit

Owning a Machine Gun: All citizens without license or permit, must abide federal law

Carrying a Loaded Firearm in Public: Unconcealed carry is unrestricted in most locations.

Traveling with Firearms: Loaded handguns can be transported in open view by any person. Handguns can be concealed if unloaded and secured in a storage compartment or case.

State Parks: Only permit carriers

Gun Possession on College Campuses: Dependent on college administration

Additional Notes and Points of Interest: South Dakota is very gun friendly. Travelers should have little trouble if he or she keeps their firearm in plain view. Additionally, individuals riding motorcycles should not travel with a loaded handgun unless they have a carry permit. Motorcyclists should keep long arms cased and unloaded.

FIREARM FRIENDLY: A+

Selective Excerpt From the State's Law:

Permit to Carry a Concealed Pistol.

An individual who wishes to carry a concealed pistol on or about his person or in a vehicle must obtain a Permit to Carry a Concealed Pistol (SDCL 22-14-9). A person does not need a permit to own a pistol, keep it in his home, business, or property, or visibly carry it (SDCL 22-14-11). Carrying a concealed pistol without a permit is a Class 1 misdemeanor, punishable by one year imprisonment or one thousand dollar fine or both (SDCL 22-14-9).

A Permit to Carry a Concealed Pistol may be obtained from the sheriff of the county of which the applicant is a resident (SDCL 23-7-7). A permit is valid for four years and the fee is $10.00 (SDCL 23-7-8.2). The applicant must complete a form called an Application and Temporary Permit to Carry a Concealed Pistol. The information required for the permit includes (SDCL 23-7-8): the applicant's complete name, address, occupation, place and date of birth, physical description, a statement that the applicant has never pled guilty to, nolo contendere to, or been convicted of a crime of violence, a sworn statement that the information on the application is true and correct, and the applicant's signature. Providing false information or false evidence of identity in applying for a permit to carry a concealed pistol is a Class 6 felony punishable by two years imprisonment, a fine of two thousand dollars, or both (SDCL 23-7-12).

The applicant must also meet the following requirements (SDCL 23-7-7.1):

18 years of age or older, never pled guilty to, nolo contendere to, or been convicted of a felony or a crime of violence, not habitually intoxicated or drugged condition, no history of violence, has not been found in the previous ten years to be a "danger to others" or a "danger to self" as defined in 27A-1-1 or is not currently adjudged mentally incompetent, has physically resided in and is a resident of the county where the application is being made for at least thirty days immediately preceding the date of the application, has had no violations of chapter 23-7 (firearms control), 22-14 (unlawful use of weapons) or 22-42 (controlled substances and marijuana) in the five years preceding the date of application or is not currently charged under indictment or information for such an offense, a citizen of the United States, and is not a fugitive from justice.

Contact for Additional Information:
South Dakota Security of State
500 East Capitol Ave./Suite 204 • Pierre, SD 57501
605-773-3537

Permit Carriers:

Concealed Carry: All citizens shall be issued a carry permit.

Unconcealed Carry: Allowed, but rare

Traveling with a Firearm: Loaded handguns and long arms may be transported on a person or in his or her vehicle. Long arms should not have a round in the chamber, but only in the magazine.

Notifying Law Enforcement of Carry Permit and Firearm: Only required if requested by an officer.

Self-Defense Model: Castle doctrine. Stand your ground.

Restaurants: Permit carriers can carry firearms in restaurants that do not have posted signs noting otherwise and as long as alcohol is not consumed.

Recognizes Carry Permits Issued by: All states

Law Uniformity: Local agencies cannot make new, additional restrictions to the state's gun law. Some laws have been grandfathered in certain areas.

All Citizens and Those Without Carry Permits:

Owning a Firearm: All citizens without license or permit

Owning a Semi-Auto: All citizens without license or permit

Owning a Machine Gun: All citizens without license or permit, must abide federal law

Carrying a Loaded Firearm in Public: Forbidden without carry permit

Traveling with a Firearm: Firearms should be kept in plain view or unloaded, and separated from ammunition and unfolded magazines also clear. Handguns should not be kept in the glove box or center console. Loaded firearms should only be transported by individuals with carry permits.

State Parks: Only permit carriers

Gun Possession on College Campuses: Forbidden

Additional Notes and Points of Interest: Tennessee is gun friendly, as it recognizes all carry permits issued by other states. Those without a carry permit are recommended to travel with their firearm unloaded, in a case, and kept in the trunk to avoid any unwanted hassle.

FIREARM FRIENDLY: A+

Selective Excerpt From the State's Law:

Some of the Qualifications of Receiving Concealed Carry Permit.

1. Effective July 1, 2005, all handgun permit applicants seeking a new permit must provide proof of U.S. Citizenship or Lawful Permanent Residency.

2. Effective July 1, 2005, Tennessee handgun carry permit law will now allow certain applicants already exempt from complying with firing range provisions of the current statute to also be exempt from any classroom requirements. Those current exceptions are applicants who prove to the department that within five (5) years from the date of application for handgun permit, the applicant has: Been certified by the police officer's standards and training commission, or successfully completed training at the law enforcement training academy; or successfully completed the firearms training course required for armed security guards; or successfully completed all handgun training of not less than four (4) hours as required by any branch of the military.

3. Applicants are required to be a resident of the State of Tennessee;

4. Be at least twenty-one (21) years of age;

5. Applicants shall not have been convicted of any felony offense punishable for a term exceeding one (1) year;

6. Applicants shall not currently be under indictment or information for any criminal offense punishable by a term exceeding one (1) year;

7. Shall not be currently the subject of any order of protection;

8. Shall not be a fugitive from justice;

9. Shall not be an unlawful user of or addicted to alcohol or any controlled substance and the applicant has not been a patient in a rehabilitation program or hospitalized for alcohol or controlled substance abuse or addiction within ten (10) years from the date of application;

Contact for Additional Information:
Tennessee Department of Public Safety
P.O Box 945 • Nashville, TN 37202
615-251-8590

Permit Carriers:

Concealed Carry: All citizens shall be issued a carry permit.

Unconcealed Carry: Largely forbidden

Traveling with a Firearm: Loaded, concealed and unconcealed firearms can be carried anywhere in a vehicle.

Notifying Law Enforcement of Carry Permit and Firearm: Immediately upon making contact with an officer. Individuals must show the officer a valid photo ID.

Self-Defense Model: Castle doctrine. Stand your ground.

Restaurants: Permit carriers can carry firearms in restaurants that do not have posted signs noting otherwise and as long as alcohol is not consumed.

Recognizes Carry Permits Issued by: All states but Maine, Minnesota, New Hampshire, Ohio, Oregon, and Wisconsin

Law Uniformity: Local agencies cannot make additional restrictions to most aspects of the state's gun law.

All Citizens and Those Without Carry Permits:

Owning a Firearm: All citizens without license or permit

Owning a Semi-Auto: All citizens without license or permit

Owning a Machine Gun: All citizens without license or permit, must abide federal law

Carrying a Loaded Firearm in Public: Forbidden

Traveling with a Firearm: Loaded handguns may be transported concealed on a person as long is the person is not committing a crime beyond a minor traffic offense. The state doesn't regulate transporting loaded long arms, which may be transported open or in a case.

State Parks: Only permit carriers

Gun Possession on College Campuses: Only permit carriers, but also dependent on school administration

Additional Notes and Points of Interest: Texas, along with Alaska and a few others, is perhaps the most gun friendly state in the country. It is remarkable and a great freedom that the state allows individuals without a carry permit to transport a loaded, concealed handgun in his or her vehicle. Individuals who are hunting and participating in shooting events may carry a loaded handgun without a permit while in transit to and from said event. Sound suppresses are allowed to be used while hunting.

FIREARM FRIENDLY: A+

Selective Excerpt From the State's Law:

GC §411.172. ELIGIBILITY (for Concealed Carry Permit).

(a) A person is eligible for a license to carry a concealed handgun if the person:

(1) is a legal resident of this state for the six-month period preceding the date of application under this subchapter or is otherwise eligible for a license under Section 411.173(a);

(2) is at least 21 years of age;

(3) has not been convicted of a felony;

(4) is not charged with the commission of a Class A or Class B misdemeanor or equivalent offense, or of an offense under Section 42.01, Penal Code, or equivalent offense, or of a felony under an information or indictment;

(5) is not a fugitive from justice for a felony or a Class A or Class B misdemeanor or equivalent offense;

(6) is not a chemically dependent person;

(7) is not incapable of exercising sound judgment with respect to the proper use and storage of a handgun;

(8) has not, in the five years preceding the date of application, been convicted of a Class A or Class B misdemeanor or equivalent offense or of an offense under Section 42.01, Penal Code, or equivalent offense;

(9) is fully qualified under applicable federal and state law to purchase a handgun;

(10) has not been finally determined to be delinquent in making a child support payment administered or collected by the attorney general;

(11) has not been finally determined to be delinquent in the payment of a tax or other money collected by the comptroller, the tax collector of a political subdivision of the state, or any agency or subdivision of the state;

(12) is not currently restricted under a court protective order or subject to a restraining order affecting the spousal relationship, other than a restraining order solely affecting property interests;

(13) has not, in the 10 years preceding the date of application, been adjudicated as having engaged in delinquent conduct violating a penal law of the grade of felony; and

(14) has not made any material misrepresentation, or failed to disclose any material fact, in an application submitted pursuant to Section 411.174.

Contact for Additional Information:
Texas Department of Public Safety
P.O. Box 4087 • Austin, TX 78773
512-424-7293

Permit Carriers:

Concealed Carry: All citizens shall be issued a carry permit.

Unconcealed Carry: Permitted only with a carry permit

Traveling with a Firearm: May transport loaded, concealed handguns in a vehicle. All long arms should remain unloaded anywhere in a vehicle.

Notifying Law Enforcement of Carry Permit and Firearm: Only required if requested by an officer.

Self-Defense Model: Castle doctrine. Stand your ground.

Restaurants: Permit carriers can carry firearms in restaurants that do not have posted signs noting otherwise and as long as alcohol is not consumed.

Recognizes Carry Permits Issued by: All states

Law Uniformity: Local agencies cannot make additional restrictions to most aspects of the state's gun law.

All Citizens and Those Without Carry Permits:

Owning a Firearm: All citizens without license or permit

Owning a Semi-Auto: All citizens without license or permit

Owning a Machine Gun: All citizens without license or permit, must abide federal law

Carrying a Loaded Firearm in Public: All citizens can carry an unconcealed handgun with an empty chamber and loaded magazine. Individuals should use discernment when doing this.

Traveling with a Firearm: Long arms must remain unloaded while handguns may be concealed or stored anywhere in a vehicle. The state defines loaded as the chamber being clear, but not necessarily the magazine.

State Parks: Only permit carriers

Gun Possession on College Campuses: Only permit carriers

Additional Notes and Points of Interest: Most establishments cannot prevent individuals from storing a firearm in their vehicle while in their parking lot. State buildings, religious establishments, and schools are the exception to this. For permit carriers, the state is one of the few that allows individuals to carry concealed firearms into primary and secondary schools.

Contact for Additional Information:
Utah Department of Public Safety
West 5400 South • Salt Lake City, UT 84129
801-965-4445

FIREARM FRIENDLY: A+

Selective Excerpt From the State's Law:

53-5-704. Bureau duties -- Permit to carry concealed firearm -- Certification for concealed firearms instructor -- Requirements for issuance -- Violation -- Denial, suspension, or revocation -- Appeal procedure.

(1) (a) The bureau shall issue a permit to carry a concealed firearm for lawful self defense to an applicant who is 21 years of age or older within 60 days after receiving an application, unless the bureau finds proof that the applicant does not meet the qualifications set forth in Subsection (2).

(b) The permit is valid throughout the state for five years, without restriction, except as otherwise provided by Section 53-5-710.

(c) The provisions of Subsections 76-10-504(1) and (2), and Section 76-10-505 do not apply to a person issued a permit under Subsection (1)(a).

(d) Subsection (4)(a) does not apply to a non-resident: (i) active duty service member, who present to the bureau orders requiring the active duty service member to report for duty in this state; or (ii) an active duty service member's spouse, stationed with the active duty service member, who presents to the bureau the active duty service member's orders requiring the service member to report for duty in this state.

(2) (a) The bureau may deny, suspend, or revoke a concealed firearm permit if the applicant or permit holder: (i) has been or is convicted of a felony; (ii) has been or is convicted of a crime of violence; (iii) has been or is convicted of an offense involving the use of alcohol; (iv) has been or is convicted of an offense involving the unlawful use of narcotics or other controlled substances; (v) has been or is convicted of an offense involving moral turpitude; (vi) has been or is convicted of an offense involving domestic violence; (vii) has been or is adjudicated by a state or federal court as mentally incompetent, unless the adjudication has been withdrawn or reversed; and (viii) is not qualified to purchase and possess a firearm pursuant to Section 76-10-503 and federal law.

(b) In determining whether an applicant or permit holder meets the qualifications set forth in Subsection (2)(a), the bureau shall consider mitigating circumstances.

(3) (a) The bureau may deny, suspend, or revoke a concealed firearm permit if it has reasonable cause to believe that the applicant or permit holder has been or is a danger to self or others as demonstrated by evidence, including: (i) past pattern of behavior involving unlawful violence or threats of unlawful violence;

(ii) past participation in incidents involving unlawful violence or threats of unlawful violence; or (iii) conviction of an offense in violation of Title 76, Chapter 10, Part 5, Weapons.

(b) The bureau may not deny, suspend, or revoke a concealed firearm permit solely for a single conviction of an infraction violation of Title 76, Chapter 10, Part 5, Weapons.

(c) In determining whether the applicant or permit holder has been or is a danger to self or others, the bureau may inspect: (i) expunged records of arrests and convictions of adults as provided in Section 77-40-109; and (ii) juvenile court records as provided in Section 78A-6-209.

Permit Carriers:

Concealed Carry: All citizens shall carry a concealed firearm, no license required

Unconcealed Carry: Accepted in most areas, no license required

Traveling with a Firearm: Individuals may transport a loaded concealed or open handgun in a vehicle. All long arms should remain unloaded in a vehicle.

Notifying Law Enforcement of Carry Permit and Firearm: Only required if requested by an officer.

Self-Defense Model: No castle doctrine.

Restaurants: Anyone without previous felony convictions may dine while carrying a handgun.

Recognizes Carry Permits Issued by: All states

Law Uniformity: Local agencies cannot make additional restrictions to most aspects of the state's gun law.

All Citizens and Those Without Carry Permits:

Owning a Firearm: All citizens without license or permit

Owning a Semi-Auto: All citizens without license or permit

Owning a Machine Gun: All citizens without license or permit, must abide federal law

Carrying a Loaded Firearm in Public: All citizens may carry a concealed or open firearm, no license required

Traveling with a Firearm: Individuals may transport a loaded concealed or open handgun in a vehicle. All long arms should remain unloaded in a vehicle.

State Parks: All those without previous felony convictions may carry a concealed weapon in a state park.

Gun Possession on College Campuses: Dependent on college administration

Additional Notes and Points of Interest: Vermont is one of the few states that does not require a permit to carry an open or concealed firearm in public. It should be noted that firearms are not permitted on any property owned or controlled by the government. Travelers will likely find traveling through Vermont to be hassle free.

Contact for Additional Information:
Attorney General of Vermont
109 State Street • Montpelier, VT 05609
802-828-3171

FIREARM FRIENDLY: A+

Selective Excerpt From the State's Law:

<u>SELECTED VERMONT LAWS GOVERNING, THE
USE AND POSSESSION OF FIREARMS.</u>

The following are selected Vermont statutes dealing with the use and possession of firearms. For a complete listing of Vermont's firearm statutes, please consult the Vermont Statutes Online, at

http://www.leg.state.vt.us/statutes/statutes2.htm.

Vermont's hunting laws and regulations can be found
at http://www.vtfishandwildlife.com/.

Title 13: Section 4003. Carrying dangerous weapons.

A person who carries a dangerous or deadly weapon, openly or concealed, with the intent or avowed purpose of injuring a fellow man, or who carries a dangerous or deadly weapon within any state institution or upon the grounds or lands owned or leased for the use of such institution, without the approval of the warden or superintendent of the institution shall be imprisoned not more than two years or fined not more than $200.00, or both.

§ 4004. Possession of dangerous or deadly weapon in a
school bus or school building or on school property

(a) No person shall knowingly possess a firearm or a dangerous or deadly weapon while within a school building or on a school bus. A person who violates this section shall, for the first offense, be imprisoned not more than one year or fined not more than $1,000.00, or both, and for a second or subsequent offense shall be imprisoned not more than three years or fined not more than $5,000.00, or both.

(b) No person shall knowingly possess a firearm or a dangerous or deadly weapon on any school property with the intent to injure another person. A person who violates this section shall, for the first offense, be imprisoned not more than two years or fined not more than $1,000.00, or both, and for a second or subsequent offense shall be imprisoned not more than three years or fined not more than $5,000.00, or both.

(c) This section shall not apply to: (1) A law enforcement officer while engaged in law enforcement duties. (2) Possession and use of firearms or dangerous or deadly weapons if the board of school directors, or the superintendent or principal if delegated authority to do so by the board, authorizes possession or use for specific occasions or for instructional or other specific purposes.

(d) As used in this section: (1) "School property" means any property owned by a school, including motor vehicles. (2) "Owned by the school" means owned, leased, controlled or subcontracted by the school. (3) "Dangerous or deadly weapon" has the meaning defined in section 4016 of this title. (4) "Firearm" has the meaning defined in section 4016 of this title. (5) "Law enforcement officer" has the meaning defined in section 4016 of this title.

(e) The provisions of this section shall not limit or restrict any prosecution for any other offense, including simple assault or aggravated assault.

GINIA

Permit Carriers:

Concealed Carry: All citizens shall be issued a carry permit.

Unconcealed Carry: Unrestricted, but not common or always permitted in metropolitan areas

Traveling with a Firearm: Loaded handguns may be transported in a vehicle for self-defense purposes. Handguns can be concealed on a person or in the glove box. Long arms should be unloaded while in transport.

Notifying Law Enforcement of Carry Permit and Firearm: Only required if requested by an officer.

Self-Defense Model: No castle doctrine. Stand your ground not accepted at some places in the state.

Restaurants: Permit carriers can carry firearms in restaurants that do not have posted signs noting otherwise and as long as alcohol is not consumed.

Recognizes Carry Permits Issued by: Alaska, Arizona, Arkansas, Delaware, Florida, Kentucky, Louisiana, Michigan, Minnesota, Mississippi, Missouri, Montana, Nebraska, New Mexico, North Carolina, North Dakota, Ohio, Oklahoma, Pennsylvania, South Carolina, South Dakota, Tennessee, Texas, Utah, Washington, West Virginia, Wyoming

Law Uniformity: Local agencies can make additional restrictions to the state's laws

All Citizens and Those Without Carry Permits:

Owning a Firearm: All citizens without license or permit

Owning a Semi-Auto: All citizens without license or permit, but ownership of USAS-12, streetsweeper shotguns, and striker 12s is prohibited

Owning a Machine Gun: The state requires a permit for machine gun ownership

Carrying a Loaded Firearm in Public: Unrestricted, but not common or always permitted in metropolitan areas

Traveling with a Firearm: Loaded handguns may be transported in open view or in a glove box or center console. Loaded long arms may be secured in gun cases, in the passenger compartment, or rear storage space.

State Parks: Only permit carriers

Gun Possession on College Campuses: Dependent on college administration

Additional Notes and Points of Interest: It should again be noted that long arms should be kept in a case and not concealed on a person. Local businesses cannot forbid their employees from keeping firearms in their vehicles.

FIREARM FRIENDLY: A+

Selective Excerpt From the State's Law:

§ 18.2-308.01. Carrying a concealed handgun with a permit.

A. The prohibition against carrying a concealed handgun in clause (i) of subsection A of § 18.2-308 shall not apply to a person who has a valid concealed handgun permit issued pursuant to this article. The person issued the permit shall have such permit on his person at all times during which he is carrying a concealed handgun and shall display the permit and a photo identification issued by a government agency of the Commonwealth or by the U.S. Department of Defense or U.S. State Department (passport) upon demand by a law-enforcement officer. A person to whom a nonresident permit is issued shall have such permit on his person at all times when he is carrying a concealed handgun in the Commonwealth and shall display the permit on demand by a law-enforcement officer. A person whose permit is extended due to deployment shall carry with him and display, upon request of a law-enforcement officer, a copy of the documents required by subsection B of § 18.2-308.010.

B. Failure to display the permit and a photo identification upon demand by a law-enforcement officer shall be punishable by a $25 civil penalty, which shall be paid into the state treasury. Any attorney for the Commonwealth of the county or city in which the alleged violation occurred may bring an action to recover the civil penalty. A court may waive such penalty upon presentation to the court of a valid permit and a government-issued photo identification. Any law-enforcement officer may issue a summons for the civil violation of failure to display the concealed handgun permit and photo identification upon demand.

C. The granting of a concealed handgun permit pursuant to this article shall not thereby authorize the possession of any handgun or other weapon on property or in places where such possession is otherwise prohibited by law or is prohibited by the owner of private property. (2013, c. 746.)

Contact for Additional Information:
Virginia State Police
P.O. Box 27472 • Richmond, VA 23261
804-674-2000

WASHINGTON

Permit Carriers:

Concealed Carry: All citizens shall be issued a carry permit

Unconcealed Carry: Unrestricted with minor exceptions

Traveling with a Firearm: Loaded handguns may be transported concealed on a person while in transit. Long arms must be kept unloaded and stored in a case or gun rack.

Notifying Law Enforcement of Carry Permit and Firearm: Only required if requested by an officer.

Self-Defense Model: No castle doctrine. Stand your ground not supported in all areas.

Restaurants: Permit carriers can carry firearms in restaurants that do not have posted signs noting otherwise and as long as alcohol is not consumed.

Recognizes Carry Permits Issued by: All states

Law Uniformity: Local agencies cannot make additional restrictions to most aspects of the state's gun law.

All Citizens and Those Without Carry Permits:

Owning a Firearm: All citizens without license or permit

Owning a Semi-Auto: All citizens without license or permit

Owning a Machine Gun: Forbidden

Carrying a Loaded Firearm in Public: Unrestricted with minor exceptions

Traveling with Firearms: Handguns should be unloaded and cased, while long arms should be unloaded and detached from loaded magazines.

State Parks: Only permit carriers

Gun Possession on College Campuses: Forbidden

Additional Notes and Points of Interest: Having a carry permit doesn't allow a permit carrier to transport a loaded long arm in his or her vehicle. Additionally, while any citizen may carry an unconcealed handgun in public, only individuals with carry permits may transport loaded handguns in their vehicles.

Contact for Additional Information:
Attorney General of Washington
P.O. Box 40100 • Olympia, WA 98504
360-753-6200

FIREARM FRIENDLY: A

WASHINGTON

Selective Excerpt From the State's Law:

How to Get Your license: Concealed Pistol License
(Courtesy of the State's Department of Licensing).

Requirements:

You must meet all of the following requirements to get
a concealed pistol license (RCW 9.41.070):

-Be 21 years of age or older at time of application.

-Have no pending trial, appeal, or sentencing on a charge
that would prohibit you from having a license.

-Have no outstanding warrants for any charge, from any court.

-Have no court order or injunction against possessing a firearm.

-Have never been adjudicated mentally defective or
incompetent to manage your own affairs.

-Have no felony convictions, or adjudications for a
felony offense, in this state or elsewhere.

-Within the past year, haven't been an unlawful user of, or addicted to,
marijuana, depressants, stimulants, narcotics, or any other controlled substance.

-Haven't been convicted of three or more violations of
Washington's firearms laws within any 5-year period.

-Haven't been dishonorably discharged from the armed forces.

-Have never renounced your United States citizenship.

-Have no convictions for any of the following crimes committed by
one family member against another: Assault IV, Coercion, Stalking,
Reckless Endangerment, Criminal Trespass in the first degree,
Violation of the provisions of a protection order or no-contact order
restraining the person or excluding the person from the residence.

Documents You Will Need.

-You will need to bring all of the following when you apply:

-Valid, government-issued photo identification

-If you don't have a Washington State driver license or ID card, you must
provide proof you have lived in the state for at least the last 90 days.

-The $52.50 fee in cash, check, or money order, payable to the law
enforcement agency where you're applying. This fee is non-refundable.

-If you are in the military, your military ID and
orders listing your station location.

Background Check Required.

-The law enforcement agency will fingerprint you and conduct a
background check before you can be issued a license.

-If you are a Washington State resident, it may take up to 30 days
to complete the background check. If you are a non-resident, it
may take up to 60 days to complete the background check.

177

ST VIRGINIA

Permit Carriers:

Concealed Carry: All citizens shall be issued a carry permit.

Unconcealed Carry: Unrestricted, but local agencies may regulate use

Traveling with a Firearm: Loaded handguns may be transported in a vehicle. Long arms should be kept unloaded while in transport.

Notifying Law Enforcement of Carry Permit and Firearm: Only required if requested by an officer.

Self-Defense Model: Castle doctrine. Stand your ground in public.

Restaurants: Permit carriers can carry firearms in restaurants that do not have posted signs noting otherwise and as long as alcohol is not consumed.

Recognizes Carry Permits Issued by: Alaska, Arizona, Arkansas, Delaware, Florida, Kentucky, Louisiana, Michigan, Minnesota, Mississippi, Missouri, Montana, Nebraska, New Mexico, North Carolina, North Dakota, Ohio, Oklahoma, Pennsylvania, South Carolina, South Dakota, Tennessee, Texas, Utah, Washington, West Virginia, Wyoming

Law Uniformity: Local agencies cannot make additional restrictions to most aspects of the state's gun law. Some grandfathered laws exist.

All Citizens and Those Without Carry Permits:

Owning a Firearm: All citizens without license or permit

Owning a Semi-Auto: All citizens without license or permit

Owning a Machine Gun: All citizens without license or permit, must abide federal law

Carrying a Loaded Firearm in Public: Unrestricted to carry an unconcealed handgun in public, but local agencies may regulate use.

Traveling with a Firearm: All firearms should be unloaded but can be carried in plain view except at night.

State Parks: Only permit carriers

Gun Possession on College Campuses: Dependent on college administration

Additional Notes and Points of Interest: It should again be noted that individuals with carry permits are not allowed to transport loaded long arms. Individuals with carry permits can keep weapons concealed in a vehicle's storage compartment.

Contact for Additional Information:
Attorney General of West Virginia
State Capitol Bldg. 1, Room 26E • Charleston, WV 25305
304-558-2021

FIREARM FRIENDLY: A+

Selective Excerpt From the State's Law:

<u>FREQUENTLY ASKED QUESTIONS.</u>

QUESTION: Is a license required to carry a concealed handgun in West Virginia?

ANSWER: Yes. Any person who intends to carry a concealed handgun must obtain a license to do so. Concealed deadly weapons include pistols, revolvers, and other types of handguns and firearms. However, concealed weapon permits may only be issued for pistols or revolvers. W. Va. Code § 61-7-4(a). The only persons exempt from state licensing requirements are: law enforcement officers; on-duty correctional officers; on-duty members of the armed forces or National Guard; and certain judicial officials and employees.

QUESTION: How long is a concealed handgun license valid?

ANSWER: Five years from the date of issuance, unless sooner revoked. Licenses are valid throughout the state during the five-year period.

QUESTION: What if my license is revoked?

ANSWER: Your license will be revoked if you violate or become unable to meet any of the licensing application requirements. You must immediately surrender your license to the issuing sheriff when you become ineligible for continued licensure.

QUESTION: Where can I apply for a concealed deadly weapons license?

ANSWER: At the office of the sheriff in your county of residence. A list of sheriff's offices is in this booklet.

QUESTION: How much does a license cost?

ANSWER: You pay $75.00 to the sheriff at the time you apply. If your application is approved, you pay an additional $25.00 prior to issuance of the license for the State Police background check.

QUESTION: What are the training requirements to obtain a license?

ANSWER: Before filing your concealed weapons licensing application, you must present evidence that you have successfully completed one of the following training courses in handling and firing a handgun: 1) Any National Rifle Association ("NRA") handgun safety or training course; 2) Any handgun safety or training course available to the public through an official law enforcement organization or an educational institution; 3) Any handgun safety or training course conducted by an instructor certified by the state or by the NRA; 4) Any handgun safety or training course conducted by the U.S. military, reserves, or National Guard. An applicant must present a photocopy of a certificate of course completion, an affidavit from the instructor, or some other document which verifies successful training course completion in order to obtain a license.

Permit Carriers:

Concealed Carry: All citizens shall be issued a carry permit.

Unconcealed Carry: Unrestricted across the state for anyone with or without a carry permit

Traveling with a Firearm: Loaded handguns can be transported in a vehicle. Long arms should be kept unloaded and stored in a trunk or rear compartment of a vehicle.

Notifying Law Enforcement of Carry Permit and Firearm: Only required if requested by an officer.

Self-Defense Model: Castle doctrine. Stand your ground only permitted in vehicles.

Restaurants: Permit carriers can carry firearms in restaurants that do not have posted signs noting otherwise and as long as alcohol is not consumed.

Recognizes Carry Permits Issued by: Arizona, Arkansas, California, Colorado, Connecticut, Georgia, Hawaii, Idaho, Indiana, Iowa, Kansas, Kentucky, Louisiana, Maryland, Michigan, Minnesota, Montana, Nebraska, New Mexico, New York, North Carolina, North Dakota, Pennsylvania, Tennessee, Texas, Utah, non-resident permits from Virginia, West Virginia (issued offer after 06/08/12), Washington, Wyoming, Puerto Rico, U.S. VI

Law Uniformity: Local agencies cannot make additional restrictions to the state's gun law.

All Citizens and Those Without Carry Permits:

Owning a Firearm: All citizens without license or permit

Owning a Semi-Auto: All citizens without license or permit

Owning a Machine Gun: All citizens without license or permit, must abide federal law

Carrying a Loaded Firearm in Public: Unrestricted across the state for anyone with or without a carry permit.

Traveling with a Firearm: Loaded handguns should be stored in a trunk or rear compartment of a vehicle, out of reach from passengers. Long arms should be kept unloaded and stored in a trunk or rear compartment of a vehicle.

State Parks: Only permit carriers

Gun Possession on College Campuses: Permit for any gun owner

Additional Notes and Points of Interest: Loaded handguns cannot be concealed while on an ATV, boat, or any assorted motor craft. Non-permit carriers taking unconcealed handguns into public should ensure the gun is kept on a visible side holster. The state allows loaded magazines to be kept anywhere in a vehicle.

FIREARM FRIENDLY: A+

Selective Excerpt From the State's Law:

CONCEALED CARRY AND FIREARMS LAWS IN WISCONSIN
(Courtesy of the State's Legislative Reference Bureau).

INTRODUCTION.

2011 Wisconsin Act 35 authorized eligible residents, effective November 1, 2011, to be licensed to carry a concealed weapon such as a handgun. In general, the Wisconsin Department of Justice must issue a concealed carry license to any resident applicant over 21 years of age who is not prohibited under state or federal law from possessing a firearm. Applicants must submit proof of firearms training and undergo a criminal history background check. Under the law, all weapons, including concealed firearms, are prohibited in certain places such as courthouses and police stations. In addition, proprietors of businesses and other property owners may post signs to prohibit people from carrying a firearm on their premises and governments may prohibit persons from carrying a firearm in all or parts of public buildings except parking areas.

Wisconsin joined 48 other states that have explicitly authorized various levels of concealed carry permitting or do not prohibit going armed with concealed weapons in public. Illinois is the only state that completely bans concealed carry. However, a federal appeals court ruled in December 2012, that Illinois would have to allow ordinary citizens to carry weapons outside their homes in certain circumstances.

Training Requirements.

An applicant must provide a certificate or proof of training, which may be met by any of the following:

-The Department of Natural Resources (DNR) Hunter Safety program or similar qualified course from another jurisdiction.

-Firearms safety or training course taught by a certified or qualified instructor offered by a national or state organization, by a law enforcement agency, or by a technical college or other post-secondary educational institution, a firearms training school, or any other qualified instructor.

-Documentation that a person completed military, law enforcement, or security training that gave the person experience with firearms; or documentation of completion of military small arms training as demonstrated by an honorable discharge or general discharge under honorable conditions or a certificate of completion of basic training with a service record of successful completion of small arms training and certification.

-A current or expired license (or a photocopy) that the person holds or has held that indicates the person is licensed or has been licensed to carry a firearm in Wisconsin or in another state or in a county or municipality of Wisconsin or another state, unless the license has been revoked for cause.

Contact for Additional Information:
Attorney General of Wisconsin
P.O. Box 7857 • Madison, WI 53707
608-266-1221

Permit Carriers:

Concealed Carry: All citizens shall be issued a carry permit.

Unconcealed Carry: Unrestricted and generally accepted

Traveling with a Firearm: Loaded handguns may be transported on a person or anywhere in a vehicle. Long arms may not be concealed on one's person.

Notifying Law Enforcement of Carry Permit and Firearm: Only required if requested by an officer.

Self-Defense Model: Castle doctrine. Stand your ground not accepted at some locations in the state.

Restaurants: Permit carriers can carry firearms in restaurants that do not have posted signs noting otherwise and as long as alcohol is not consumed.

Recognizes Carry Permits Issued by: Alabama, Alaska, Arizona, Arkansas, Colorado, Florida, Georgia, Idaho, Indiana, Iowa, Kentucky, Louisiana, Maine, Michigan, Minnesota, Mississippi, Missouri, Montana, Nebraska, New Hampshire, Ohio, North Carolina, North Dakota, Oklahoma, Pennsylvania, South Carolina, South Dakota, Tennessee, Texas, Utah, Virginia, West Virginia

Law Uniformity: Local agencies cannot make additional restrictions to most aspects of the state's gun law.

All Citizens and Those Without Carry Permits:

Owning a Firearm: All citizens without license or permit

Owning a Semi-Auto: All citizens without license or permit

Owning a Machine Gun: All citizens without license or permit, must abide federal law

Carrying a Loaded Firearm in Public: Unrestricted and generally accepted for individuals with and without a carry permit to carry a loaded, unconcealed handgun in public.

Traveling with a Firearm: Individuals who are non-residents can transport loaded firearms in plain view or anywhere in a vehicle if the gun is cased. Those 21 years of age or older can carry a concealed handgun anywhere in a vehicle. Long arms may not be concealed on a person and should be cased or kept in a gun rack.

State Parks: Only permit carriers

Gun Possession on College Campuses: Dependent on college administration.

Additional Notes and Points of Interest: The state only permits concealed carry to individuals with a carry permit. Individuals without their carry permit must keep their handgun on visible belt holsters or in plain view in their vehicle.

FIREARM FRIENDLY: A+

Selective Excerpt From the State's Law:

<u>WYOMING CONCEALED FIREARM STATUTE.</u>

(Note: Yellow highlight provided to denote modified areas of the statute effective 07-01-2011.)6-8-104. Wearing or carrying concealed weapons; penalties; exceptions; permits.

The attorney general through the division shall issue a permit

(i) Is a resident of the United States and has been a resident of Wyoming for not less than six (6) months prior to filing the application;

(ii) Is at least twenty-one (21) years of age;

(iii) Does not suffer from a physical infirmity which prevents the safe handling of a firearm;

(iv) Is not ineligible to possess a firearm pursuant to 18 U.S.C. section 922(g) or W.S. 6-8-102;

(v) Has not been: (A) Committed to a state or federal facility for the abuse of a controlled substance, within (B) Convicted of a felony violation of the Wyoming Controlled Substances Act of 1971, the one (1) year period to the date on which application for a permit under this section is submitted; W.S. 35-7-1001 through 35-7-1057 or similar laws of any other state or the United States relating to controlled substances and has not been pardoned; or 1971, W.S. 35-7-1001 through 35-7-1057 or similar laws of any other state or the United States relating to controlled substances within the one (1) year period to the date on which application for a permit under this section is submitted normal faculties are impaired. (etc.)

(vi) Does not chronically or habitually use alcoholic liquor and malt beverages to the extent that his normal faculties are impaired.

(vii) Demonstrates familiarity with a firearm. A legible photocopy of a certificate of completion of shall constitute evidence of qualification under this paragraph.

Contact for Additional Information:
Attorney General of Wyoming
208 S. College Dr. • Cheyenne, WY 82002
307-777-7181

After reading this book, you should feel confident carrying a concealed weapon in public. Owning firearms and carrying concealed handguns is one of the greatest freedoms Americans enjoy. Because of the unparalleled level of safety these guns provide, we hope future generations of Americans have the right to carry concealed weapons just as we can today. Unfortunately, certain groups and political factions seem bent on stripping Americans of the right to bear arms and more specifically the right to carry concealed weapons. These skeptics have allowed themselves to believe guns only exist to cause harm and fail to realize firearms —especially concealed handguns— help ensure bad things don't happen to good people. Good people require very little governing, but, regardless how many laws our government passes, bad people will continue to act on their own malicious accord. By carrying a concealed handgun, a person can protect their right to life and wellbeing from those bent on evil and wrongdoing.

We'd encourage you to engage in civil discourse concerning both local and national gun laws. Politicians become less likely to vote for anti-gun bills if their constituents make it clear they wish to retain their rights to own and carry firearms. Alongside politicians, you could also politely discuss the benefits of guns ownership with your co-workers, family, friends and neighbors, helping them realize guns, when used responsibly, are nothing to fear. Anyone carrying a concealed weapon should also do so responsibly, as to not give fodder to those wishing to ban firearms. Each time an individual with their concealed carry license misuses their weapon, it strengthens the argument for those who'd like to see firearms out of civilian hands. We, as those carrying concealed weapons, must police ourselves and only use our firearm when lives are at stake. If we use our guns for self-defense and within the confines of the law, we'll further guarantee Americans retain the right to carry weapons for generations to come.